THE AWKWARD OPTIMIST

A FIELD MANUAL FOR THE SOCIALLY AMBITIOUS

HECTOR M. RODRIGUEZ

"BECAUSE EVEN YOUR MOST EMBARRASSING
SOCIAL FAILURES CAN BECOME YOUR BEST
STORIES—IF YOU LIVE TO TELL THEM."

"The Awkward Optimist's Guide to Human Connection—A Field Manual for the Socially Ambitious"
First Edition
Copyright © 2025 Hector M Rodriguez

Library of Congress Cataloging-in-Publication Data

Rodriguez, Hector M
"The Awkward Optimist's Guide to Human Connection—A Field Manual for the Socially Ambitious" / Hector M. Rodriguez
p. cm.

ISBN: 978-1-7355584-8-6 (Paperback)
ISBN: 978-1-7355584-9-3 (eBook)

1. Self-Help Adult 2. Humor 3. Social Fabric Human Connection
Printed in United States of America
First Printing: January 2025
For permissions requests, email the author/publisher at:
hcsm@comcast.net

Book Design: Marie Stirk

DISCLAIMER

10 9 8 7 6 5 4 3 2 1

ADDITIONAL WORKS BY THE AUTHOR

What Happened to Joe French?

The Path Taken:
A Father and Son Journey on the Camino de Santiago

24 Stories- A Collection of Shorts

A Story

24 More—A Collection of Shorts

Echoes of Awakening

The Awkward Optimist's Guild to Human Connection
(A Field Guide to the Socially Ambitious)

TABLE OF CONTENTS

DEDICATION

TO ALL THE WONDERFULLY AWKWARD SOULS who've ever stumbled over their words, tripped on their own feet, and somehow, miraculously, found connection amidst the chaos. This book is dedicated to you. May your future interactions be filled with less cringe and more genuine laughter. And may your pickup lines, even the disastrous ones, become legendary tales told with a twinkle in your eye and a hearty chuckle. Because let's face it, the most memorable moments are often the ones that go hilariously wrong. So go forth, embrace the absurdity, and know that even the most epic social fails are just stepping-stones on the path to becoming a master of human interaction (or at least a more entertaining version of yourself). To the perpetually optimistic, to the relentlessly clumsy, to the eternally hopeful: you are not alone. This book is proof.

PREFACE

SO, YOU'RE HOLDING this book. Congratulations! You've officially taken the first step (beyond the awkward shuffle and mumbled greeting) towards improving your social life, one hilarious anecdote at a time. Maybe you're hoping to conquer the art of the pickup line, maybe you just enjoy a good cringeworthy story, or maybe you're simply intrigued by the bizarre science of human interaction. Whatever your reason, welcome aboard this slightly chaotic, yet hopefully insightful, journey.

This book isn't your grandma's stuffy self-help manual (unless your grandma has a wicked sense of humor and a penchant for observational comedy). We'll delve into the psychology of attraction, yes, but we'll do it with the kind of witty banter you'd expect from a particularly clever group of friends dissecting a particularly disastrous dating app profile. Expect relatable anecdotes, insightful commentary, and a healthy dose of self-deprecating humor. After all, who better to guide you through the minefield of social interactions than someone who's accidentally set off every alarm along the way?

Remember, this book is not a foolproof guide to social perfection. Perfection is, frankly, boring. Embrace the awkwardness, learn from the cringe, and, most importantly, laugh at yourself along the way. The goal isn't flawless execution; it's building genuine connections and having a little fun while doing it. Let's begin!

INTRODUCTION

LET'S BE HONEST, the world of meeting people can be a bit of a minefield. One wrong step, one misplaced word, and suddenly you're trapped in a conversation about the weather (the ultimate social purgatory). But fear not, intrepid social explorer! This book is your survival guide—your witty compass and insightful map—through the sometimes-treacherous terrain of human interaction.

Forget those stuffy self-help books that preach about "authenticity" and "emotional intelligence" in monotone. This is a different kind of adventure. We're diving headfirst into the hilarious, often cringeworthy world of making connections, dissecting the science and art of social success (and spectacular failure) with a healthy dose of humor and irreverence.

We'll explore the anatomy of the perfect (and utterly disastrous) pickup line, analyze the unspoken language of body language, and investigate the surprising psychology behind what makes us click (or not click) with someone. We'll examine real-life scenarios—from the slightly awkward encounter at the museum to the slightly more chaotic bar scene—and analyze what worked (and what spectacularly didn't). Think of it as a crash course in social skills, but with significantly more laughs and significantly fewer inspirational quotes.

So, grab a beverage, settle in, and prepare to laugh, learn, and maybe even improve your odds of avoiding the dreaded "friend zone"—or at least survive it with your sense of humor intact. This isn't just a book; it's a journey. And while I can't guarantee you'll emerge as the ultimate social butterfly; I can guarantee a good amount of entertainment along the way. Let the adventures begin!

CHAPTER 1
THE SCIENCE OF THE AWKWARD

DECODING SOCIAL INTERACTIONS

THE ANATOMY OF A PICKUP LINE
A POSTMORTEM

LET'S DISSECT the pickup line—that tiny, fragile vessel of hope carrying the weight of your romantic aspirations (or, at the very least, a mildly interesting conversation). It's a delicate dance of words, a high-wire act performed above the chasm of potential rejection. And boy, oh boy, have I seen some spectacular falls.

First, let's address the elephant in the room—the sheer audacity of the pickup line. It's a bold declaration of intent, a social gamble with odds that are, let's be honest, often stacked against you. It's a bit like walking into a lion's den armed with nothing but a feather duster and a prayer. But every now and then, a daring adventurer emerges victorious. The question is: what separates the winners from the losers in this verbal jungle?

The anatomy of a successful pickup line is a fascinating study in subtle cues, strategic word choice, and the elusive art of reading the room. It's not just what you say, but how you say it. Consider the context. A cheesy line that might work in a boisterous pub might fall utterly flat in a quiet library. Imagine attempting a "Do you believe in love at first sight, or should I walk by again?" line in the hallowed halls of a museum—the librarian's glare alone could melt the polar ice caps.

Word choice is crucial. Avoid clichés like the plague. "Are you a parking ticket? Because you've got 'fine' written all over you" is, frankly, insulting to both the recipient and the English language. This line falls into the "try-hard" category—a desperate attempt to be clever that often backfires spectacularly. The recipient isn't impressed by your attempts at wit; they're wondering if you've ever actually had a genuine conversation in your life.

Authenticity is key. A genuine compliment, delivered with sincerity, is far more effective than any rehearsed line. Notice something specific about the person—their unique style, a fascinating piece of jewelry, a book they're reading. Comment on it. Show genuine interest. "That's a really interesting book; I've heard great things about it," is infinitely more engaging than a tired old line. It indicates you're observant, you're curious, and that you're interested in them as an individual, not just a potential conquest.

Delivery is everything. Confidence is attractive. Nerves are understandable, but they shouldn't paralyze you. If you're a nervous wreck, it will show.

Practice your approach in the mirror, or with a trusted friend. Remember, the goal isn't to flawlessly execute a memorized line; it's to initiate a conversation. Think of it as a warm-up, a way to break the ice and transition into genuine interaction.

Let's explore some case studies of pickup line success and failure. One particularly cringe-worthy attempt I witnessed involved a man at a coffee shop attempting a line based on the person's drink. "You like that latte? So do I, which means we have something in common, and destiny brought us together. We're meant to be!" The woman's response? A polite, but firm, "No, thank you" followed by a quick retreat into the safety of her newspaper. The cringe factor alone was enough to make me spill my own beverage. The line was overly effusive and lacked any genuine personal connection—it was essentially a formulaic attempt at romance that failed to account for basic human connection.

Conversely, I once observed a wonderfully understated approach. A man in a bookstore simply complimented a woman on her choice of books. "I've always wanted to read that one—I've heard amazing things about it." He didn't attempt a witty one-liner, he simply engaged in a common interest. This led to a conversation about literature, a shared passion, and eventually, a date. This is the power of genuine connection. This line worked because it was authentic, specific, and respectful.

Understanding context is also important. A line that works in a lively, bustling environment might fall completely flat in a more subdued setting. Imagine trying a playful quip in a quiet library—the librarian's glare alone would be a sufficient deterrent. Equally, a deep and meaningful line might feel awkward in a casual setting where light-hearted banter is the norm.

Consider the power of observation. Before launching into your verbal assault (or charming overture), take a moment to assess the situation. Is the person engaged in a conversation? Are they clearly preoccupied? Respect their space and their time. If they look busy, respect their focus and don't interrupt. A well-timed approach is as crucial as the words themselves. An interruption, on the other hand, can be a sure-fire recipe for disaster.

Humor, when used appropriately, can be a great tool. But the humor has to be genuine and relevant. Avoid anything that could be construed as offensive or disrespectful. The goal is to make them laugh, not to make them uncomfortable or feel degraded. A self-deprecating joke can be a good icebreaker but avoid anything that's overly self-critical or overly reliant on stereotype.

Let's analyze some common pitfalls. Overly confident lines, designed to impress rather than connect, often backfire. Lines that are too long, too complicated, or overly rehearsed feel unnatural and inauthentic. And lines that are based on assumptions about the person you are talking to run a higher risk of coming across as insensitive or even offensive. The key to creating an effective approach is not necessarily the content of the opening line, but rather the intention behind it. Does your attempt show that you've considered the person as an individual? Or is it just a rehearsed, repetitive template for picking up someone?

Finally, remember the golden rule of social interaction: be respectful. Rejection is a possibility, and it's okay. Learn from any awkward encounters and move on. Don't take it personally. Some people may not be looking for connection; some may not be interested in you. That's fine. The world is full of potential connections.

The art of the pickup line, therefore, isn't about memorizing a list of clever lines, it's about cultivating a genuine interest in others, developing the ability to read social cues, and practicing the art of confident, respectful communication. It's about understanding that a failed attempt is simply a learning opportunity, and that genuine connection is far more valuable than any perfectly crafted line. So, go forth, armed with your newfound knowledge. But remember, the most important ingredient is always authenticity. And maybe a little bit of humor, if you can pull it off. Just keep the feather duster handy, you never know when you might need it.

BEYOND THE ONE LINER
THE ART OF CONVERSATION
STARTERS

SO, YOU'VE SUCCESSFULLY navigated the treacherous waters of the initial approach—you've uttered your meticulously crafted (or hilariously improvised) opening line. Congratulations! You've survived the first hurdle. But the game, my friend, is far from over. We're now entering the complex, often baffling, and frequently hilarious realm of nonverbal communication. This isn't just about decoding subtle shifts in posture; it's about mastering the art of reading the room (and the person) like a seasoned poker player, except instead of chips, the stakes are your social standing—and maybe a date.

Forget those cheesy self-help books promising to unlock the secrets of the universe with a simple eyebrow raise. The truth is far more nuanced, far messier, and infinitely more amusing. Nonverbal communication isn't a precise science; it's a chaotic dance of subtle gestures, fleeting expressions, and subconscious cues that can leave even the most experienced social butterflies feeling utterly bewildered.

Let's start with the basics. Imagine you've just launched into a fascinating anecdote about your pet hamster's escape from its cage (yes, truly fascinating—trust me). Your potential conversational partner's eyes are glazing over, their body subtly shifting away, perhaps even a slight yawn escapes—despite the hamster's heroic (and arguably hair-raising) adventure. These are not signs of a soul enthralled by your storytelling prowess. These are clear signals that your hamster saga, while epic in your mind, is less than enthralling to them.

But what about the opposite? How do you spot the signs of genuine engagement? Well, unlike the hamster escape scenario, look for active listening cues. This isn't just about them sitting quietly; it's about engaged quietness. Think: leaning slightly forward, maintaining eye contact (but not in a creepy, staring way—think friendly, interested contact), nodding subtly to show understanding, and maybe even mirroring your body language. Mirroring is a subconscious behavior that often indicates connection—subtly mimicking your posture or gestures shows that they're subconsciously attuned to you and possibly finding you engaging.

Facial expressions, however, are a whole other

ballgame. A genuine smile reaches the eyes—it's called the Duchenne smile, named after the French neurologist who first identified it—it's much harder to fake than a simple lip curl. A real smile crinkles the corners of the eyes, creating those endearing little crow's feet. A fake smile? Well, it's usually just a lip-twitching affair, lacking the genuine warmth and twinkle in the eyes that mark authentic delight. So, pay attention to those tiny details; they often speak volumes.

But body language is more than just smiles and eye contact. Consider posture. An open, relaxed posture—arms uncrossed, shoulders relaxed, body facing towards you—indicates receptiveness and comfort. Conversely, a closed-off posture—arms crossed, shoulders hunched, body turned away—signals disengagement, discomfort, or even defensiveness. This doesn't necessarily mean they dislike you; it could simply mean they're feeling overwhelmed, nervous, or just not comfortable in the specific situation. Remember to consider context, always!

Then there's the matter of touch. This is a delicate area, so tread lightly! An accidental brush of hands can spark an unexpected connection (or a terrified retreat, depending on the context and your delivery). However, be mindful; unwanted touching is a major social faux pas that can quickly derail any budding conversation. The key here is reading the situation and understanding the social cues. If you're unsure, err on the side of caution—perhaps save the shoulder rub for a slightly later stage of the relationship, when you have a better sense of their comfort level.

And let's not forget the power of silence—or, more specifically, the type of silence. A comfortable silence, shared between two people who are engaged and finding each other's company pleasant, is drastically different from the awkward, deathly silence punctuated only by the nervous clicking of your own teeth.

A comfortable silence often feels pregnant with unspoken understanding, almost as if words are unnecessary. An awkward silence, on the other hand, feels like an eternity of unspoken anxieties, heavy with the weight of unrealized expectations. It's a silence filled with the phantom sounds of crickets chirping loudly in your ears, a mental soundtrack only you can hear. It's the silence that makes you want to spontaneously combust. Learning to distinguish between these two kinds of silences is crucial to navigating the social labyrinth.

Now, let's dive into some more specific examples, because sometimes, theory only gets you so far. Picture this: you're at a coffee shop, attempting to engage in conversation with someone who seems equally captivated by the intricacies of your artisanal latte foam. However, despite your best efforts, their eyes keep darting towards the exit, their body language is tense, and they keep checking their watch. Despite your witty banter about the merits of oat milk versus almond milk (a debate far more fascinating than it sounds), they're clearly not engaged, and frankly, they're probably already mentally composing an escape plan.

Let's take another scenario. You're at a party, surrounded by a cacophony of chatter and questionable music choices, and you've finally found someone who seems genuinely interested in your conversation. They lean in when you speak, their eyebrows raise when you make a funny observation, and their smile is not only genuine but incredibly infectious. They might even lightly touch your arm to emphasize a point, creating a connection that feels both natural and comfortable. This is the kind of body language that tells you your conversational gambit has succeeded; you've cracked the code.

However, reading nonverbal cues isn't a magic trick. It requires practice, observation, and a willingness to accept that you will make mistakes—and sometimes, those mistakes will be hilariously awkward. The key is to be observant, to pay attention to the subtle nuances of body language, to consider the context, and to be flexible.

Remember, people aren't robots. They don't always express themselves perfectly clearly, and neither do we. Sometimes, a crossed arm might simply mean they're cold, not that they're actively rejecting you. Sometimes, a lack of eye contact might indicate shyness, not disinterest. Context is crucial, and a little bit of empathy goes a long way.

Ultimately, mastering nonverbal communication is about building a skill set that transcends rote memorization of signals. It's about cultivating a sensitivity to the emotional landscape of social interactions, developing an awareness of subtle cues, and learning to react with grace (and hopefully humor) when things inevitably go sideways. So, keep practicing, keep observing, and remember: the journey itself, filled with its share of awkward silences and misinterpreted gestures, is half the fun. And if all else fails, remember the feather duster. You'll never know when it might come in handy.

READING THE ROOM AND
THE PERSON'S NONVERBAL CUES

SO, YOU'VE SUCCESSFULLY navigated the treacherous waters of the initial approach—you've uttered your meticulously crafted (or hilariously improvised) opening line. Congratulations! You've survived the first hurdle. But the game, my friend, is far from over. We're now entering the complex, often baffling, and frequently hilarious realm of nonverbal communication. This isn't just about decoding subtle shifts in posture; it's about mastering the art of reading the room (and the person) like a seasoned poker player, except instead of chips, the stakes are your social standing—and maybe a date.

Forget those cheesy self-help books promising to unlock the secrets of the universe with a simple eyebrow raise. The truth is far more nuanced, far messier, and infinitely more amusing. Nonverbal communication isn't a precise science; it's a chaotic dance of subtle gestures, fleeting expressions, and

17

subconscious cues that can leave even the most experienced social butterflies feeling utterly bewildered.

Let's start with the basics. Imagine you've just launched into a fascinating anecdote about your pet hamster's escape from its cage (yes, truly fascinating—trust me). Your potential conversational partner's eyes are glazing over, their body subtly shifting away, perhaps even a slight yawn escapes—despite the hamster's heroic (and arguably hair-raising) adventure. These are not signs of a soul enthralled by your storytelling prowess. These are clear signals that your hamster saga, while epic in your mind, is less than enthralling to them.

But what about the opposite? How do you spot the signs of genuine engagement? Well, unlike the hamster escape scenario, look for active listening cues. This isn't just about them sitting quietly; it's about engaged quietness. Think: leaning slightly forward, maintaining eye contact (but not in a creepy, staring way—think friendly, interested contact), nodding subtly to show understanding, and maybe even mirroring your body language. Mirroring is a subconscious behavior that often indicates connection—subtly mimicking your posture or gestures shows that they're subconsciously attuned to you and possibly finding you engaging.

Facial expressions, however, are a whole other ballgame. A genuine smile reaches the eyes—it's called the Duchenne smile, named after the French neurologist who first identified it—it's much harder to fake than a simple lip curl. A real smile crinkles the corners of the eyes, creating those endearing little crow's feet. A fake smile? Well, it's usually just a lip-twitching affair, lacking the genuine warmth and twinkle in the eyes that mark authentic delight. So, pay attention to those tiny details; they often speak volumes.

But body language is more than just smiles and eye contact. Consider posture. An open, relaxed posture—arms uncrossed, shoulders relaxed, body facing towards you—indicates receptiveness and comfort. Conversely, a closed-off posture—arms crossed, shoulders hunched, body turned away—signals disengagement, discomfort, or even defensiveness. This doesn't necessarily mean they dislike you; it could simply mean they're feeling overwhelmed, nervous, or just not comfortable in the specific situation. Remember to consider context, always!

Then there's the matter of touch. This is a delicate area, so tread lightly! An accidental brush of hands can spark an unexpected connection (or a terrified retreat, depending on the context and your delivery). However, be mindful; unwanted touching is a major social faux pas that can quickly derail any budding conversation. The key here is reading the situation and understanding the social cues. If you're unsure, err on the side of caution—perhaps save the shoulder rub for a slightly later stage of the relationship, when you have a better sense of their comfort level.

And let's not forget the power of silence—or, more specifically, the type of silence. A comfortable silence, shared between two people who are engaged and finding each other's company pleasant, is drastically different from the awkward, deathly silence punctuated only by the nervous clicking of your own teeth.

A comfortable silence often feels pregnant with unspoken understanding, almost as if words are unnecessary. An awkward silence, on the other hand, feels like an eternity of unspoken anxieties, heavy with the weight of unrealized expectations. It's a silence filled with the phantom sounds of crickets chirping loudly in your ears, a mental soundtrack only you can hear. It's the silence that makes you want to spontaneously combust. Learning to distinguish between these two kinds of silences is crucial to navigating the social labyrinth.

Now, let's dive into some more specific examples, because sometimes, theory only gets you so far. Picture this: you're at a coffee shop, attempting to engage in conversation with someone who seems equally captivated by the intricacies of your artisanal latte foam. However, despite your best efforts, their eyes keep darting towards the exit, their body language is tense, and they keep checking their watch. Despite your witty banter about the merits of oat milk versus almond milk (a debate far more fascinating than it sounds), they're clearly not engaged, and frankly, they're probably already mentally composing an escape plan.

Let's take another scenario. You're at a party, surrounded by a cacophony of chatter and questionable music choices, and you've finally found someone who seems genuinely interested in your conversation. They lean in when you speak, their eyebrows raise when you make a funny observation, and their smile is not only genuine but incredibly infectious. They might even lightly touch your arm to emphasize a point, creating a connection that feels both natural and comfortable. This is the kind of body language that tells you your conversational gambit has succeeded; you've cracked the code.

However, reading nonverbal cues isn't a magic trick. It requires practice, observation, and a willingness to accept that you will make mistakes—and sometimes, those mistakes will be hilariously awkward. The key is to be observant, to pay attention to the subtle nuances of body language, to consider the context, and to be flexible.

Remember, people aren't robots. They don't always express themselves perfectly clearly, and neither do we. Sometimes, a crossed arm might simply mean they're cold, not that they're actively rejecting you. Sometimes, a lack of eye contact might indicate shyness, not disinterest. Context is crucial, and a little bit of empathy goes a long way.

Ultimately, mastering nonverbal communication is about building a skill set that transcends rote memorization of signals. It's about cultivating a sensitivity to the emotional landscape of social interactions, developing an awareness of subtle cues, and learning to react with grace (and hopefully humor) when things inevitably go sideways. So, keep practicing, keep observing, and remember: the journey itself, filled with its share of awkward silences and misinterpreted gestures, is half the fun. And if all else fails, remember the feather duster. You'll never know when it might come in handy.

THE PERILS OF SMALL TALK NAVIGATING THE SHALLOW WATERS

HAVING SUCCESSFULLY LAUNCHED your verbal torpedo (or perhaps a more subtle, yet equally effective, conversational icebreaker), you find yourself adrift in the often-treacherous waters of small talk. Congratulations! You've survived the initial assault, only to find yourself facing a seemingly endless expanse of polite pleasantries and the ever-present threat of awkward silence. Fear not, intrepid conversationalist! This is where the real test begins—the subtle art (and science) of navigating the shallows, avoiding the conversational reefs, and hopefully, reaching the calmer waters of genuine connection.

Small talk, often dismissed as meaningless chatter, is actually a surprisingly complex social ritual. It's the conversational equivalent of a carefully choreographed dance, requiring precise timing, delicate footwork (metaphorically speaking, of course), and a keen awareness of your partner's rhythm and mood. Get it wrong, and you risk a sudden, jarring halt to the proceedings. Get it right, and you pave the way for something deeper, something... more.

One of the most common perils of small talk is the dreaded "weather report." We've all been there—trapped in a conversational vortex of meteorological minutiae, discussing the subtle nuances of precipitation or the surprisingly intense debate regarding the precise shade of grey of a particularly overcast sky. While the weather is a universally understood topic, its conversational value quickly diminishes. It's the conversational equivalent of a beige wall—safe, but utterly devoid of personality or intrigue. Unless, of course, you're discussing the impending arrival of a category 5 hurricane, in which case, small talk is likely the least of your concerns.

Another treacherous pitfall is the conversational equivalent of a minefield—the politically charged topic. Unless you're meticulously analyzing the seismic shifts in global politics with a seasoned diplomat, steer clear of controversial subjects. Discussions on religion, politics, and the merits of pineapple on pizza are best reserved for those with a well-established rapport and a high tolerance for passionate disagreement (and possibly burnt pizza). Remember, the goal is connection, not conflict.

Then there's the infamous "one-upper." This is

the individual who transforms every anecdote into a competition, turning your mildly interesting story of a slightly delayed flight into an epic tale of a harrowing week-long journey through a war-torn nation. While their experiences might be fascinating, the conversational dynamic shifts from a shared exchange to a performance—a subtle but significant power play. Engage with a one-upper and you risk becoming a mere prop in their grand narrative, their life experiences overshadowing yours. It's a fine line—showing genuine interest while politely declining the invitation to compete in a conversational Olympics.

Mastering the art of small talk requires a certain degree of improvisation. It's about being responsive, attentive, and capable of gracefully pivoting from one topic to another. It's not about sticking to a rigid script; it's about adapting to the ebb and flow of the conversation, detecting subtle shifts in your partner's interest, and steering away from potentially awkward or divisive waters. Think of it as freestyle conversational kayaking—navigating the currents of conversation with grace and agility.

One strategy to enhance your small talk skills is to hone your active listening abilities. This is more than simply hearing the words; it involves engaging with the speaker's message, demonstrating genuine interest, and responding thoughtfully. This involves more than just nodding your head or uttering the occasional "uh-huh." Ask follow-up questions, show genuine curiosity, and reflect their emotions—all while avoiding the uncanny valley of excessive mirroring, which can come off as bizarrely robotic.

Body language plays a significant role in small talk. Open posture, appropriate eye contact, and subtle mirroring of your partner's gestures can significantly enhance rapport. However, excessive mirroring or overly intense eye contact can create unease and discomfort. Strive for a balance—be present and engaged without being overly intrusive. Imagine it's a delicate dance—a waltz of conversational engagement, not a tango of intense scrutiny.

Humor, when used appropriately, can be a powerful tool in navigating the intricacies of small talk. A well-placed joke or a witty observation can break the ice, lighten the mood, and create a sense of connection. But caution is advised! Humor is subjective, and what one person finds hilarious, another may find offensive or simply dull. Know your audience and gauge their sense of humor before unleashing your arsenal of comedic witticisms.

In the realm of small talk, self-awareness is paramount. Pay attention to your own conversational habits—are you prone to interrupting? Do you monopolize the conversation? Are you overly self-conscious? Recognizing your own conversational tendencies can help you identify areas for improvement. Record yourself engaging in conversations, if you're feeling brave, and analyze your performance with a critical (yet compassionate) eye.

And finally, remember the art of the graceful exit. Sometimes, despite your best efforts, the conversation simply stagnates or veers into uncomfortable territory. Learning to gracefully extricate yourself from an unproductive or awkward conversation is a crucial skill. A polite excuse—"Excuse me, I need to grab a drink," or "It was lovely chatting with you, I'm going to catch up with a friend"—is sufficient. Avoid lengthy explanations or apologies; a simple, polite exit is always best.

Small talk, though seemingly trivial, is a fundamental building block of social interaction. Mastering this art isn't merely about avoiding awkward silences; it's about fostering connections, building rapport, and demonstrating your social intelligence. It is a skill honed over time, through practice, observation, and a healthy dose of self-awareness. So, embrace the challenge, navigate those conversational currents with grace and humor, and remember: even the most seasoned conversationalists have experienced their fair share of awkward moments. It's all part of the delightfully messy journey of human connection.

Think of small talk as a game of conversational Jenga. Each statement is a block, carefully placed to build a structure of engagement. One wrong move, one misplaced word, and the whole thing could come crashing down. The key is to build slowly, carefully, observing the overall balance of the conversation, and anticipating potential points of collapse. It's a delicate process, requiring patience, skill, and a healthy dose of luck.

Beyond the technical skills, remember that the heart of successful small talk lies in genuine interest in the other person. Let curiosity be your compass. Focus on what the other person is saying, demonstrating active listening, and showing genuine engagement. Ask open-ended questions that invite thoughtful responses rather than simple "yes" or "no" answers. The goal is to build a connection, not just to fill the silence.

Imagine you're exploring a new and fascinating land—the landscape of another person's experiences and perspectives. Each conversation is a journey, and your role is that of a curious traveler, eager to explore and discover new things. Let your genuine curiosity guide you, and you'll find that navigating the often-challenging terrain of small talk becomes less of a chore and more of an adventure.

Furthermore, remember that small talk is not just about what you say, but also about what you don't say. Sometimes, silence can be a powerful tool. A well-timed pause can create space for reflection, allowing both parties to process information and formulate a thoughtful response. It's the conversational equivalent of a perfectly placed musical rest—creating a sense of anticipation and anticipation. Don't be afraid of silence; sometimes, it's the most eloquent statement of all.

Finally, remember that everyone experiences awkward moments in social interactions. It's part of the human condition. Don't let the fear of awkwardness paralyze you. Embrace the awkward moments; learn from them, and let them be a source of both self-awareness and amusement. After all, what's life without a few delightfully cringe-worthy moments? Small talk, like life itself, is a journey filled with ups and downs, unexpected turns, and moments of both brilliance and utter absurdity. Embrace the ride.

ZERO TO HERO
BUILDING RAPPORT AND
CONNECTION

SO, YOU'VE NAVIGATED the perilous shoals of the initial greeting. You've dodged the conversational torpedoes of forced laughter and escaped the quicksand of uncomfortable silences. Congratulations, you're still standing! But the journey to genuine connection is far from over. Think of it less like scaling Everest and more like navigating a particularly challenging escape room filled with cryptic clues, unexpected obstacles, and the ever-present threat of a sudden, inexplicable power outage. This is where the real magic—and the real challenge—begins: building rapport.

Building rapport isn't about mastering some secret handshake or reciting lines from a cheesy pickup artist manual. It's about creating a genuine connection, a sense of understanding and mutual respect.

It's about making the other person feel seen, heard, and valued—like you genuinely want to know them, not just their shoe size or the make of their car. This is where the psychology gets interesting, because it's less about what you say and more about how you make the other person feel.

One of the most crucial elements of rapport-building is active listening. Now, this isn't the kind of listening where you're mentally composing your witty rebuttal while the other person is describing their weekend trip to see their aunt Mildred's prize-winning petunias. Active listening involves truly paying attention, not just to the words being spoken, but also to the nonverbal cues—the subtle shifts in body language, the tone of voice, the unspoken emotions lurking beneath the surface. It's like being a detective, piecing together clues to unravel the mystery of the person sitting across from you. Are they enthusiastic about their aunt Mildred's petunias? Or is that just a polite way of shifting the conversation? Your skills of observation will tell you.

Mirroring and matching, a technique borrowed from the world of behavioral psychology, can subtly enhance rapport. This doesn't mean you become a bizarre mimic, echoing every gesture and facial expression. Instead, it's about subtly aligning your body language with theirs. If they lean forward, you might subtly do the same. If they speak slowly and deliberately, you might adjust your pace to match. It's a subconscious signal of connection, a silent affirmation that you're on the same wavelength. Think of it as a carefully choreographed dance where the steps are not perfectly matched but rather move in harmony.

Finding common ground is another key ingredient. This isn't about pretending to love opera if you secretly find it excruciatingly boring. It's about identifying shared interests, experiences, or values. Did they mention a love of vintage sci-fi movies? Great! You can casually mention your own obsession with "Battlestar Galactica," thus creating a bridge of shared enthusiasm. Did they mention their dog? Well, unleash your inner dog lover (even if you're secretly a cat person—professional courtesy). This is where being a good observer during the initial stages comes in handy, picking up clues to build this common ground. Don't force it; let it evolve organically.

Remember, conversation isn't a competition. It's a collaborative effort. Avoid the temptation to dominate the conversation, turning it into a monologue showcasing your impressive knowledge of obscure historical facts or your ability to flawlessly recount the plot of "Casablanca." Give the other person ample opportunity to speak, ask them open-ended questions, and truly listen to their answers. Open-ended questions such as "What was the most memorable part of your trip?" are infinitely better than ones that only permit "Yes" or "No" answers, such as, "Did you have fun?" These open-ended questions invite detailed and engaging responses, making the interaction far more rewarding for both parties.

And let's not forget the power of empathy. Putting yourself in the other person's shoes, trying to understand their perspective, even if you don't necessarily agree with it, is a powerful way to build connection. Empathy goes beyond simply listening; it's about actively trying to understand their feelings and experiences. Even if they're complaining about the latest episode of their favorite reality show, showing empathy can transform a mundane conversation into a meaningful exchange.

Humor, used judiciously, can be a powerful tool for building rapport. But remember, humor is subjective. What one person finds hilarious, another might find offensive or simply bewildering. Avoid anything that could be interpreted as insensitive or offensive, particularly regarding race, religion, politics, or anything else that could be considered highly personal. Instead, opt for self-deprecating humor or observations about shared human experiences. Think witty anecdotes, clever observations, or even a well-timed, self-aware awkward pause. This is where a good sense of self-awareness is crucial, as is understanding your audience. You wouldn't joke about your love of reality TV shows with a physics professor known for his disdain for popular culture.

And finally, remember the importance of being

yourself. Trying to be someone you're not is exhausting and ultimately ineffective. Authenticity is attractive. People are drawn to genuineness, to someone who isn't afraid to be themselves, quirks and all. Embrace your imperfections, your eccentricities, your delightful awkwardness. It's those unique traits that make you, well, you. And that's something worth celebrating.

The process of building rapport isn't a sprint; it's a marathon. It takes time, patience, and genuine effort. There will be stumbles, awkward silences, and moments when you wonder if you've accidentally stepped into a time warp and are now conversing with a particularly opinionated potted plant. But with practice, observation, and a willingness to be truly present, you can master the art of connection, transforming those potentially awkward encounters into genuine, meaningful relationships.

Consider this analogy: Imagine you're trying to assemble a complex piece of furniture—say, a Victorian-era chaise lounge. The instructions are cryptic, the parts are numerous, and the risk of accidentally creating a bizarre, unusable monstrosity is high. Building rapport is similar. There are no simple, foolproof instructions. The "parts"—the nonverbal cues, the shared experiences, the empathetic responses—must be carefully assembled, mindful of the individual context. Sometimes you'll have extra pieces you don't know where to put. Sometimes a piece will break, requiring a repair of your strategy. The process will be iterative. But with patience and attention, you'll slowly assemble a solid structure, and the end result will be a connection that's far more rewarding than any pre-fabricated piece of furniture you can buy.

The journey from zero to hero in the realm of social interaction isn't about becoming a charismatic superstar who effortlessly charms everyone they meet. It's about cultivating genuine connections, built on mutual respect, understanding, and a healthy dose of self-awareness. It's about accepting the awkward moments, learning from them, and, yes, even laughing at them. Because, let's face it, life—and social interaction—are far more interesting when seasoned with a healthy dose of delightful absurdity. So, go forth, intrepid conversationalist, and embrace the chaos! The world is waiting to be connected—one awkward, hilarious, and ultimately rewarding conversation at a time. And don't forget to bring your sense of humor! You'll need it.

CHAPTER 2
THE ZOO, THE BAR,
AND THE MUSEUM

PICKUP LINES IN THE WILD

SAFARI OF THE SOUL
MEETING PEOPLE IN UNEXPECTED PLACES

LET'S BE HONEST, the dating world is a jungle. A veritable Serengeti of awkward encounters, missed connections, and the occasional spectacularly cringe-worthy pickup line. But unlike your average safari, this one takes place not in the African plains, but in the surprisingly fertile hunting grounds of... well, everywhere. We've already tackled the bar scene—a boisterous watering hole of potential partners and potential disasters. Now, let's explore the less obvious, more unexpected locales where love (or at least a mildly interesting conversation) can blossom.

Think of your social life as a meticulously planned expedition. You're not just stumbling around hoping for a gazelle of a partner to magically appear. You're strategically positioning yourself in areas with a high probability of encountering fellow humans who might share your interests—or at least your sense of humor. And the key to a successful safari of the soul? Preparation, adaptability, and a healthy dose of self-deprecation. Because let's face it, even the most seasoned adventurer stumbles occasionally.

The zoo, for instance, presents a unique set of challenges. It's a place where people are often pre-occupied with the antics of penguins or the majestic roar of a lion. Trying to wedge a conversation into that scenario requires a level of audacity bordering on genius. A simple, "Are those flamingos actually that pink in person?" might be a better opener than attempting a witty line about your own "wild" nature. The key here isn't a dazzling pick-up line; it's finding common ground in shared wonder at nature's oddities. If they're equally mesmerized by the sloth's languid movements, you've struck gold. If they're more interested in the overpriced hot dog stand, well, maybe stick to observing the animals.

Museums, on the other hand, offer a quieter, more contemplative atmosphere. This isn't the place for boisterous pronouncements of love; it's a sanctuary for more subtle approaches. Leaning in to whisper your appreciation of a particular artwork can be far more effective than shouting across the room. Choosing a piece that inspires a shared emotional response ("Isn't this portrait remarkably haunting?") is a much better strategy than launching into a debate about the artist's technique (unless, of course, you're both art historians—then, by all means, delve into the nuances of post-impressionism). The goal here is shared appreciation, not a forced conversation. Let the art act as a conversational springboard; then gracefully transition into other shared interests.

Libraries, those hushed havens of knowledge, might seem like an unlikely place to find romance, but they offer a great opportunity for authentic connection. Observe someone reading a book that piques your interest. A simple, "That's a fascinating book; I've always wanted to read it," can be a charming and non-threatening opening. This approach is far less likely to be perceived as intrusive than some loud, bar-room pickup line. The library setting implicitly suggests a shared intellectual curiosity—an excellent foundation for a connection. Remember to keep your voice down and maintain the library's respectful atmosphere. You don't want to be shushed mid-conversation!

But the unexpected locations don't stop there. Consider a farmers' market, teeming with local produce and potential partners. You could strike up a conversation about the best way to ripen avocados, debate the merits of heirloom tomatoes, or simply compliment someone's taste in artisanal cheeses. These organic conversations flow from shared interests, avoiding the forced nature of many pickup lines. The key is genuine curiosity, not a pre-rehearsed script.

Even seemingly mundane places like coffee shops or bookstores can become fertile grounds for connection. You could ask for a recommendation, comment on a book cover, or simply engage in a friendly exchange about the weather. These everyday encounters, unlike planned nights out, offer a less-pressurized environment for interactions. The key is to remain natural and engaging. It's about building a connection through shared experience, rather than through a perfectly crafted line.

The beauty of these unexpected locales lies in their authenticity. You're not trying to play a role or impress someone with a witty line; you're simply being yourself, engaging with your surroundings and the people within them. This genuineness is disarming, creating a more relaxed and natural environment for connection. It's about shared experiences and genuine interest—and that's far more attractive than any pickup line could ever be.

Let's consider the psychology behind this approach. Instead of relying on a pre-programmed line designed to impress, you're leveraging the power of shared context. You're creating a common ground, a shared experience that acts as a natural conversation starter. This fosters a sense of connection, bypassing the initial awkwardness often associated with forced interactions.

Furthermore, this approach eliminates the pressure of performing. There's no need to be witty or charming; instead, you focus on genuine engagement. This removes the element of artifice, allowing your true personality to shine through. And genuine personality is always more alluring than a perfectly crafted line.

Think about it: what's more memorable, a smooth line about a person's eyes or a shared moment of laughter over a particularly unusual vegetable at the farmers market? The latter is far more likely to foster a genuine connection, built on shared experience and mutual interest, rather than a fleeting moment of impressed amusement.

The key to this safari of the soul isn't about finding the perfect place or the perfect line. It's about being open to the unexpected, embracing the awkwardness, and finding common ground in the most unlikely of places. It's about recognizing opportunities for connection and approaching them with genuine curiosity and a sense of humor. And remember: even if the conversation fizzles, you've gained a unique experience and a potentially hilarious anecdote for your next social gathering. Consider it a successful expedition, even without a romantic conquest—after all, even a fruitless safari yields valuable observations about the wild world of human interaction. And that, my friend, is a priceless reward in itself.

The real adventure isn't about finding "the one" instantly. It's about embracing the process, learning from your experiences, and honing your social skills along the way. Each encounter, successful or not, provides valuable lessons in navigating the complex landscape of human connection. So, pack your metaphorical bags, equip yourself with a sense of humor and a dash of courage, and embark on your own safari of the soul. You might be surprised at the fascinating creatures (and potential partners) you encounter along the way. The journey itself, with all its twists, turns, and occasional near-misses with awkwardness, is the real reward. Enjoy the wild ride!

THE WATERING HOLE
NAVIGATING THE BAR SCENE

THE BAR. Ah, the bar. A place of shimmering possibilities, potent cocktails, and the potential for both epic triumphs and spectacular failures in the art of human connection. It's a social ecosystem all its own, a swirling vortex of dimly lit corners, sticky floors, and the ever-present hum of conversation punctuated by the clinking of glasses. Navigating this terrain requires a delicate balance of confidence, wit, and a healthy dose of self-awareness—lest you become another cautionary tale whispered amongst the bartenders.

Let's start with the basics: the approach. Forget the cheesy lines you saw on that questionable dating website. Those are the equivalent of wearing a neon sign that screams, "I'm desperately trying too hard." Instead, focus on genuine interaction. Observe the environment. Who seems approachable? Who's already engaged in conversation? Who's nursing a drink alone, silently judging the entire human race? (That last one might be a challenge, but hey, you never know!)

The "accidental" bump-in is a classic, but execute it poorly, and you'll be remembered as the clumsy oaf who spilled someone's cosmopolitan. Timing is everything. Don't interrupt a deep, meaningful conversation. Instead, wait for a natural pause, a lull in the action, a moment where your target seems open to interaction. Then, approach with a smile, make eye contact, and—here's the crucial part—actually say something.

And what to say? Forget the rehearsed lines. Start with something simple, observational, and genuine. "This place is packed tonight, huh?" or "That's quite a unique cocktail; what's in it?" These are non-threatening conversation starters. They invite a response and allow you to gauge their personality. Avoid topics that are overly personal or potentially controversial—religion, politics, exes—at least initially. Keep the conversation light and engaging. Ask open-ended questions. Listen more than you talk (a shocking revelation, I know, but bear with me). This isn't a competition; it's a conversation.

However, let's address the elephant in the room—or rather, the elephant wearing a sequined dress and swaying precariously to the thumping bass: the dreaded pickup line. While I vehemently discourage the cheesy variety, the skillful deployment of a well-crafted, witty line can actually work wonders. The key is originality and context. A line that bombs in a dive bar might slay in a sophisticated cocktail lounge. Let's dissect some examples, separating the wheat from the chaff:

The Chaff:

- "Is your name Google? Because you've got everything I've been searching for." (Cringeworthy. Overused. Predictable. Avoid at all costs.)

- "Are you a parking ticket? Because you've got 'fine' written all over you." (This one is so bad it's almost impressive in its awfulness.)

- "If you were a vegetable, you'd be a cute-cumber." (Please, no.)

The Wheat (with a healthy dose of caution):

- "I couldn't help but notice your... [mention something specific, positive, and non-intrusive, like a unique accessory or a charming smile]. I'm [your name]." (This is a classic for a reason; it's genuine, direct, and avoids cliché.)

- (Approaching someone laughing with friends) "You guys seem to be having a blast. Mind if I join the party for a bit?" (Playful, confident, and invites them to include you.)

- (Observing someone reading a book) "That's an

interesting choice! I've always been curious about [the book's genre]. What's it about?" (Shows genuine interest and provides a jumping-off point for a meaningful conversation.)

The crucial element is authenticity. If you're not comfortable with a particular line, it will show. Your body language will betray your insincerity, and your attempt will likely fail miserably. Confidence is key, but genuine confidence. The kind that comes from being comfortable in your own skin, rather than the bravado of someone desperately seeking validation.

Beyond the lines themselves, consider your body language. Maintain good eye contact, offer a genuine smile, and relax your shoulders. Avoid crossing your arms—this creates a barrier. Be mindful of personal space; don't invade their bubble, but also don't stand so far away that you seem disinterested.

And what about the all-important follow-up? If the conversation flows naturally, and you both seem interested, suggest grabbing another drink together, or perhaps moving to a less crowded area. If there's no spark, that's okay, too. Politely excuse yourself and move on. There are plenty more fish in the sea (or, in this case, in the bar).

Finally, remember the bar is not a battlefield. It's a social gathering place. Go with the intention of having fun, meeting new people, and maybe even forging a connection. Don't put undue pressure on yourself.

Approach each interaction with a sense of humor and lightness. If it works, great! If not, learn from the experience, dust yourself off, and try again. The bar scene is a marathon, not a sprint. And remember, even the most spectacular failures often make for the best stories. So raise a glass to the adventure, to the awkward encounters, and to the sheer, unadulterated absurdity of it all. Cheers!

Now, let's address a few specific scenarios you might encounter in the wild west of the bar scene:

- **Scenario 1:** *The Group Hangout:* Approaching a group can be daunting, but it's often more rewarding. Instead of focusing on one person, engage the entire group with a lighthearted comment or question. If they seem receptive, you can then focus on one individual for a more one-on-one conversation. But be mindful not to hog the limelight; be respectful of their group dynamic.

- **Scenario 2:** *The Shy Wallflower:* Some people need a little more coaxing. Start with a non-intrusive approach, maybe a simple compliment or a question related to their surroundings. Be patient, gentle, and respectful of their personal space. Forcing a conversation with someone who clearly isn't interested is a surefire recipe for disaster.

- **Scenario 3:** *The Overly-Confident Casanova (or Cassandra):* Be wary of individuals who are overly aggressive or try to dominate the conversation. While confidence is attractive, arrogance is a major turn-off. If someone is making you uncomfortable, politely excuse yourself. Your safety and well-being are paramount.

- **Scenario 4:** *The Accidental Spill:* Mistakes happen. If you accidentally spill someone's drink, apologize profusely, offer to buy them a replacement, and try to salvage the situation with humor and genuine remorse. This demonstrates maturity and grace under pressure—qualities that are surprisingly attractive.

- **Scenario 5:** *The "Friend Zone" Trap:* Sometimes, despite your best efforts, you might find yourself relegated to the friend zone. This is a complex situation that requires careful navigation. The key is to be honest with yourself about your feelings and intentions. If you're still interested, let the person know, while respecting their boundaries. If not, gracefully accept the friendship and move on.

The bar scene, like life itself, is a mix of successes and failures. It's a learning experience, a testing ground for social skills, and a surprisingly good source of anecdotal material for future storytelling. So embrace the chaos, laugh at the awkward moments, and remember that even the most disastrous pickup attempt can be a hilarious story later on. The journey, with all its unpredictable twists and turns, is what makes it worthwhile. Now go forth, and conquer (or at least, try to charm) the bar.

THE QUIET CORNER
APPROACHING PEOPLE IN LESS
OBVIOUS PLACES

LEAVING THE BOISTEROUS BAR scene behind, we venture into the quieter corners of social interaction—places where the pressure is lower, but the potential for genuine connection is surprisingly high. Think libraries, museums, even the surprisingly fertile ground of a well-stocked bookstore. These aren't the usual hunting grounds for the pickup artist, but for those seeking something beyond a fleeting encounter, they offer a distinct advantage: shared interests.

The key to approaching someone in these less obvious places lies in observing, engaging, and subtly weaving yourself into the conversation, rather than launching into a pre-rehearsed routine. Forget the cheesy lines; authenticity is your secret weapon here. At a museum, for instance, don't just point at a painting and declare, "That's my spirit animal!" (Unless it's a particularly expressive sloth, in which case, go for it.) Instead, observe what they're looking at, and offer a thoughtful comment. Something like, "That use of light is incredible, isn't it? I've always been fascinated by how artists manipulate light and shadow." This demonstrates shared interest and invites them to engage in a meaningful conversation, rather than a superficial exchange.

Let's take the library, for example. This hallowed hall of hushed whispers and towering shelves might seem an unlikely place for romance to bloom, but it holds untapped potential. Picture this: you're browsing the poetry section, and you spot someone engrossed in a collection of Emily Dickinson's work. Resist the urge to dramatically whisper, "Is that... Hope is the thing with feathers?" Instead, after a moment of observation (don't stalk!), casually approach. Perhaps you could comment on a specific poem, or even inquire about their thoughts on Dickinson's overall style. The key here is to show you've genuinely engaged with the same material, sparking a conversation rooted in shared intellectual curiosity.

The bookstore, a similar haven of literary treasures, offers a wealth of conversational starting points. Observe what books someone is examining. If they're poring over a first edition of a classic you adore, it's your golden ticket. A simple, "I've always loved that edition—the binding is exquisite," could easily lead to a vibrant discussion about favorite authors, reading habits, and perhaps, even a shared love for the smell of old paper. Again, focus on genuine engagement. Don't fake interest in a genre you despise just to start a conversation. Your enthusiasm (or lack thereof) will be instantly detectable.

But what if you're not a bookworm? Don't despair! These spaces offer other avenues for subtle connection. Perhaps you notice someone struggling to reach a book on a high shelf. Offering a helping hand is not only chivalrous (or, for those of us who are less chivalrous, simply helpful), but it provides a natural icebreaker. A simple "Need a hand with that?" followed by a brief, engaging comment about the book itself ("That's a fascinating subject; I've always wondered about...") can build a quick connection.

Even seemingly mundane locations hold unexpected possibilities. I once met a fascinating woman while waiting in line at the DMV. Yes, the DMV! The shared misery of bureaucratic tedium created an odd sense of camaraderie, and a seemingly absurd comment about the Kafkaesque nature of the waiting room led to a lively conversation. The point is, you can find conversation starters anywhere; it's all about embracing the unexpected and finding common ground.

Now, let's address the elephant in the room (or, in this case, the elephant in the library): rejection. It happens. It's part of the process. Remember, not every conversation will lead to a blossoming romance,

and that's perfectly okay. The goal isn't always to secure a date; it's to practice your social skills, build
confidence, and, perhaps, even make a new friend.

If someone isn't receptive, don't take it personally.
Politely excuse yourself and move on. The world is
full of people, and it's highly unlikely that you'll connect with everyone you meet. Consider it a valuable
lesson learned, and move onto the next opportunity for connection. Rejection is not an indictment
of your worth; it's simply a signal that you're not a
match for that specific person.

Another critical aspect of approaching people
in quieter environments is respecting their space.
Avoid overly loud or intrusive behavior. Maintain
a respectful distance and be mindful of their body
language. If they seem preoccupied or uninterest-
ed, gracefully withdraw. Your goal is to connect, not
to overwhelm. This is particularly crucial in places
designed for quiet contemplation, like libraries and
museums. Think of yourself as a fellow visitor, not
a predator.

Finally, remember to be yourself. Trying to be
someone you're not is exhausting and ultimately
unproductive. Authenticity is magnetic. People are
drawn to genuine enthusiasm and passion. So, approach these quieter spaces with curiosity, respect,
and a willingness to connect on a deeper level, and
who knows? You might just find something truly special—and certainly far more rewarding than

another forced smile and a tired "Hey, how's it going?" in a crowded bar. The quiet corners of life are often where the most interesting conversations begin.

Let's explore a few more specific examples. Imagine you're in a specialty coffee shop, known for its unique brewing methods. You notice someone studying the menu intently. Instead of a generic "Nice place, huh?", try something like, "I've been meaning to try their Ethiopian Yirgacheffe. Have you had it before? What do you think?" This demonstrates engagement with the shop's unique selling proposition, providing a natural entry point into a conversation.

Or perhaps you're at a botanical garden, surrounded by lush greenery. You see someone sketching a particularly striking flower. A simple "That's beautiful! I've always admired the way artists capture the delicate details of nature," is far more engaging than a cheesy pick-up line. Observe, comment, and let the conversation unfold naturally.

Even seemingly trivial events can be used to your advantage. Let's say you're at a farmers' market, and you both reach for the last heirloom tomato. A playful, "Looks like we're both fans of the perfect tomato," can open the door to a lighthearted conversation that could lead to something more. The key is to find those shared interests and leverage them to spark a meaningful exchange.

The art of connecting with people in less obvious places isn't about manipulation; it's about genuine engagement and mutual respect. It's about finding common ground, and engaging in conversation that is both enjoyable and memorable. So, the next time you're looking to make a connection, remember to look beyond the usual haunts. You might be surprised at what you find in the quieter corners of the world. The rewards, both in terms of personal connection and hilarious stories to tell later, are far more significant than anything found in a crowded bar or club. And who knows, maybe you'll even discover a new favorite place to browse antique maps, or discover a hidden talent for identifying rare orchids. The possibilities are truly endless, and far more intriguing than you might imagine.

ONLINE TO OFFLINE
BRIDGING THE GAP

SO, YOU'VE MASTERED the art of the witty online exchange. Your profile picture is impeccable (or at least, strategically filtered), your bio is a masterpiece of self-deprecating humor and subtle bragging, and your messages are a symphony of charm and cleverness. Congratulations! You've successfully navigated the treacherous waters of online dating—or at least, the initial, relatively shallow end of the pool. Now comes the real challenge: the leap from digital flirtation to the unpredictable, often terrifying, reality of an in-person encounter.

This is where many a digital Romeo and Juliet meet their untimely demise. The carefully crafted persona, the perfectly timed emojis, the witty banter that flowed effortlessly across the screen—all of it can crumble like a stale biscuit under the weight of awkward silence and the harsh glare of reality. Suddenly, that sparkling profile picture is just a slightly less blurry version of a person standing awkwardly in front of you, and your carefully constructed narrative starts to feel... contrived.

The truth is, the online world is a curated version of ourselves. We present the highlights, the best angles, the most flattering filters—both literally and figuratively. We get to edit, delete, and rewrite until we've crafted the perfect digital self. But in person, there's no delete button. There's no backspace key to correct a clumsy phrase or awkward laugh. You are, quite literally, on display. And that can be... intimidating.

One of the biggest pitfalls is the expectation gap. We build up this idealized image of the person based on limited information and often embellished profiles. We project our hopes and desires onto them, creating a fantasy that's almost inevitably going to clash with the reality of a flawed, complex human being—a reality that includes things like bad breath, slightly-off fashion choices, and the occasional unexpected burp. Let's be honest, nobody's perfect, not even the person who's been crafting the perfect online persona.

So how do we bridge this gap? How do we translate the effortless charm of online communication into the messy, unpredictable world of face-to-face interaction? It's less about perfecting a script and more about embracing the inherent awkwardness. Because let's face it, a little awkwardness is a sign that you're actually human, and that's far more appealing than some robotic, perfectly polished version of yourself.

First, manage expectations. Remember that you are meeting a human being, not a meticulously crafted online avatar. They will have flaws, quirks, and moments of awkwardness just like you. Embrace this. It's the very essence of human connection. The goal isn't to be perfect; it's to be real, relatable, and genuine.

Second, pre-date planning is crucial. Avoid the dreaded "Let's just grab a coffee" trap. Coffee shops are great, but they often lead to brief, strained conversations and quick goodbyes. Plan an activity that allows for natural interaction and shared experience. A walk in the park, a visit to a museum (avoid the overly quiet sections), a casual game of mini-golf—anything that breaks the ice and provides conversational fodder. The activity itself serves as a buffer against the pressure of maintaining continuous, flawless conversation.

Third, prepare some conversation starters that are relevant to the planned activity, but don't rely on them too heavily. If you're going to a museum, you could start with a comment about a particular piece of art ("I've always been fascinated by Impressionism, what do you think of this one?") rather than resorting to a tired pickup line that's probably been used a million times. But also be ready to deviate—sometimes the most memorable conversations stem from unexpected tangents and shared discoveries.

Fourth, be mindful of body language. This is where the online world and the offline world diverge most drastically. Online, you have time to craft your perfect response; in person, your body language speaks volumes before you even utter a word. Maintain eye contact (but don't stare!), offer a warm smile (a genuine one, not a creepy one), and keep your body language open and inviting. Avoid crossing your arms, fidgeting excessively, or looking at your phone.

Fifth, actively listen. The art of conversation is about more than just talking; it's about truly listening and engaging with what the other person has to say. Ask follow-up questions, show genuine interest in their responses, and avoid interrupting. This is also a good way to gauge their personality and assess compatibility—something that's a lot harder to do in the often-truncated exchanges of online communication.

Sixth, accept the possibility of rejection gracefully. Not every connection will work out. Sometimes, the chemistry just isn't there, and that's okay. Rejection is a part of life, and it's a valuable learning experience, even if it feels embarrassing at the time. Move on, learn from the experience, and try again. The world (and the dating pool) is vast and full of other people.

Finally, remember the humor. A little self-deprecating humor can go a long way in diffusing any awkwardness. Don't be afraid to laugh at yourself, and don't be afraid to acknowledge the slightly ridiculous nature of the whole situation. Remember that awkward moments are often the most memorable—especially the ones you can laugh about later.

Transitioning from online interactions to real-world encounters is a skill that takes practice. It requires self-awareness, emotional intelligence, and a healthy dose of resilience. But it's also an opportunity to develop stronger social skills, learn how to connect with people on a deeper level, and experience the joys and challenges of genuine human interaction, all while creating hilarious anecdotes for your future memoirs. So, take a deep breath, step outside your digital comfort zone, and embrace the delightfully chaotic world of offline connections. The rewards (and the stories) are well worth the effort. You might even discover that real-life interactions are far more rewarding—and significantly less prone to accidentally sending a message to your mother instead of your date—than the carefully curated world of online dating. And that, my friends, is a win in itself. Just remember to brush your teeth beforehand. Seriously.

FAILURE IS AN OPTION AND SOMETIMES FUNNY LEARNING FROM MISTAKES

LET'S FACE IT: the path to mastering the art of the pickup line—or, more broadly, the art of connecting with others—is paved with more than just good intentions. It's littered with the hilarious wreckage of failed attempts, awkward silences that could rival the Grand Canyon in their vastness, and enough cringe-worthy moments to fuel a stand-up comedy routine for a decade. But fear not, aspiring conversationalists! These epic fails aren't evidence of your inherent unworthiness; they're crucial steppingstones on your journey to becoming a social butterfly (or at least, a slightly less awkward caterpillar).

Think of your social interactions as a scientific experiment. Each attempt, successful or not, provides valuable data. Did your meticulously crafted pickup line fall flatter than a week-old pancake?

Analyze why! Was it too cheesy? Too aggressive? Too obscure? Perhaps your delivery lacked the necessary pizzazz, or maybe you accidentally stepped on the other person's toes (literally or metaphorically). Each failed attempt offers a chance to refine your technique, to tweak your approach, and to emerge, phoenix-like, from the ashes of embarrassment, wiser and more socially adept.

For instance, I once attempted a charmingly witty (in my own mind) pickup line at a museum dedicated to taxidermied animals. My masterpiece? "Are you a stuffed animal? Because you're looking awfully lifelike..." The response? A stony silence, followed by a rapid retreat to the opposite end of the gallery. The sheer awfulness of it still makes me wince. However, instead of letting this defeat me, I dissected the failure. The setting was inappropriate—museums, generally, aren't the ideal breeding grounds for romantic encounters (unless you're into discussing the mating rituals of the three-banded armadillo). And the line itself? Let's just say it had all the subtlety of a foghorn in a library.

Another time, armed with what I considered to be a suave and sophisticated line—"Is your name Google? Because you've got everything I've been searching for"—I approached a woman at a wine-tasting event. The response was a polite but firm "No," followed by an even more polite, but undoubtedly swift, exit. My analysis? While the line might work in certain contexts (perhaps in a highly caffeinated, low-pressure environment where people are already feeling a little light-headed), a wine-tasting event, with its atmosphere of refined taste and quiet contemplation, was clearly not the place. The lesson? Context is king. A line that might work wonders in a lively bar can flop spectacularly in a hushed library, or in the midst of trying to discuss the merits of a particular vintage.

The beauty of these failures is that they are inherently funny. Looking back, the sheer audacity of some of my pickup line attempts makes me laugh out loud. The image of me, confidently (or perhaps delusionally) delivering my cheesy line, only to be met with blank stares or polite escapes, is a comedy sketch waiting to happen. Embrace the absurdity! Laugh at yourself, learn from your mistakes, and use these experiences to fuel your future interactions.

Remember, rejection doesn't mean you're inherently flawed; it simply means that particular approach wasn't a match for that particular person, at that particular time. It's a matter of probability and chemistry, of finding the right fit. It's like trying to find the right key to unlock a door; you won't always get it right on the first try, but with persistence and a willingness to learn, you'll eventually find the one that opens the door to new connections and experiences.

And let's not forget the power of observation. Pay attention to what works and what doesn't work for others. Watch how successful people navigate social interactions. Notice their body language, their tone of voice, their ability to engage in meaningful conversations. Mimic what you admire, adapt their techniques to your own style, and avoid the pitfalls that you observe in others.

Learning from your mistakes doesn't just apply to pickup lines; it applies to all aspects of social interaction. Did you dominate a conversation, leaving others feeling unheard? Did you come across as overly serious or aloof? Did you inadvertently offend someone with a careless remark? Each of these experiences provides an opportunity for self-reflection and growth. The key is to approach these failures with a sense of humor and a willingness to learn, to see them not as setbacks but as valuable lessons.

Consider keeping a "failure journal"—a place where you can document your mishaps, analyze what went wrong, and brainstorm strategies for improvement. You'll not only gain valuable insights into your social skills but also create a hilarious record of your journey. Imagine rereading this journal years from now, chuckling at your past blunders and marveling at how far you've come. This journal will be a testament to your resilience, your growth, and your ability to laugh at yourself, all essential qualities for navigating the sometimes-chaotic world of human connection.

Moreover, remember that social skills are like

muscles; they get stronger with use. The more you practice, the more confident and adept you'll become. Don't be afraid to step outside your comfort zone, to try new approaches, and to embrace the inevitable awkward moments along the way. Each interaction, regardless of the outcome, is a valuable learning experience. And, often, the most memorable interactions are the ones that didn't quite go as planned.

Think about it: some of the funniest stories we tell are about the times we stumbled, fumbled, and completely messed up. These stories often reveal more about our character, our resilience, and our ability to laugh at ourselves than any perfectly executed social interaction could ever do. They are the ingredients of great anecdotes, the foundation for unforgettable memories, and the reminders that even in our most awkward moments, there is always something to learn and something to laugh about.

So, embrace the inevitable failures. View them as opportunities for growth, for self-discovery, and for the creation of hilarious stories that you'll be sharing for years to come. The path to social mastery is rarely a straight line; it's often a winding, bumpy road, filled with unexpected detours and the occasional spectacular crash. But with a healthy dose of self-awareness, a willingness to learn, and a hearty laugh at your own expense, you'll not only navigate these challenges, but you'll also emerge, victorious and considerably more entertaining. And who knows, maybe your next attempt will be the one that leads to a genuine connection. Or, at the very least, it'll give you a great story to tell.

CHAPTER 3
THE PSYCHOLOGY OF
ATTRACTION

WHAT MAKES THE
SPARKS IGNITE

MORE THAN JUST LOOKS
THE SCIENCE OF ATTRACTION

LET'S FACE IT, we've all been there. Standing across a crowded room, eyes locked on someone who seems to possess some sort of magical, irresistible aura. Is it the perfectly sculpted jawline? The cascade of lustrous hair? Perhaps. But let's delve a little deeper than the surface sparkle, shall we? Because the science of attraction, my friends, is far more intricate and fascinating than a simple checklist of physical attributes. It's a tangled web of psychological factors, a symphony of subconscious cues and shared experiences, all working in concert to either create a crackling connection or a deafening silence.

Forget the glossy magazine covers and the unrealistic standards perpetuated by Hollywood. While physical attractiveness undoubtedly plays a role (think initial spark, the "wow" factor), it's often the psychological underpinnings that determine whether that spark ignites into a bonfire or fizzles out like a damp firework. Think of it like this: physical attraction gets your foot in the door; psychological compatibility keeps you inside.

One of the key players in this intricate dance is something called proximity. We're far more likely to be attracted to people we encounter frequently. This isn't just a matter of convenience; it's a psychological phenomenon known as the mere-exposure effect. The more we see someone, the more familiar—and therefore, appealing—they become. So, that cute barista you see every morning? Your brain might be subtly wiring you for attraction, whether you like it or not. It's the psychological equivalent of a slow, simmering love potion.

Then there's the fascinating concept of similarity. We are drawn to people who share our values, interests, and even our quirks. It's a comforting echo of ourselves, a reassurance that we're not alone in our weirdness. This doesn't mean you need to find a carbon copy of yourself; instead, it highlights the importance of shared ground. Do you both geek out over obscure documentaries? Bond over a shared love of bad puns? Those commonalities create a foundation for connection far stronger than superficial similarities. It's the psychological glue that holds things together.

But here's where things get really interesting. Consider complementarity. While shared interests are crucial, being perfectly matched isn't always ideal.

Sometimes, opposite attracts—not in a dramatic, "I'm a chaotic artist, you're a structured accountant" way, but in a subtle, balancing act. Think of it like two puzzle pieces that fit together, not identical copies, but perfectly interlocking. One person's strengths might complement the other's weaknesses, creating a dynamic duo that's greater than the sum of its parts.

And what about those elusive qualities that we call personality traits? This is where the fun really begins. Extroversion, introversion, agreeableness, conscientiousness... the list goes on. Research shows that we're drawn to individuals who exhibit traits we admire or lack ourselves. Are you naturally shy? You might find yourself attracted to someone confident and outgoing. This isn't about seeking someone to "fix" you, but rather about finding someone who balances your personality and enhances your life experience. It's like assembling a well-rounded team.

But let's not forget the role of subconscious cues. This involves that whole "body language" thing you've probably heard about, but I'm going to give it the psychological spin it deserves. We are subconsciously picking up on tiny signals, subtle gestures and expressions that reveal far more than words ever could. A slight tilt of the head, a lingering glance, a mirrored posture—these seemingly insignificant details speak volumes about mutual interest, or lack thereof. It's a silent conversation occurring beneath the surface, a subconscious dance of attraction.

Consider the phenomenon of mirroring and matching. Have you ever noticed how, when you're genuinely connecting with someone, you might unconsciously start to mimic their body language? It's a subtle form of rapport-building, a nonverbal way of saying, "I get you." This subconscious synchronicity reinforces feelings of connection and empathy. It's like a secret handshake of the heart, a silent affirmation of shared emotional space.

And then there's reciprocity. This is the big one. Knowing that someone is genuinely interested in you is intoxicating, making you more attractive in their eyes, creating a positive feedback loop. It's the psychological version of a self-fulfilling prophecy. It's the feeling of being seen, heard, and valued—and that's alluring. It creates that magic we all long for.

Finally, let's tackle the elephant in the room: authenticity. No one's attracted to a manufactured persona. Trying to be someone you're not will always fall flat. It's exhausting, inauthentic, and ultimately, unattractive. Being your genuine self allows others to connect with the real you, flaws and all. Remember the messy, imperfect bits are part of the charm.

In short, the science of attraction isn't a simplistic equation. It's a complex interplay of physical attributes, psychological factors, and subconscious signals. It's about finding someone who not only catches your eye but resonates with your soul, someone who complements your life and makes you a better version of yourself. It's a journey of discovery, filled with laughter, awkward silences, and the occasional spectacularly failed pickup line. But remember, it's in those failures that we learn, grow, and ultimately, find the genuine connections that truly matter. So, go forth, be yourself (the wonderfully messy, imperfect you!), and embrace the beautiful, often hilarious, chaos of attraction. After all, where's the fun in predictable?

MIRRORING AND MATCHING THE SUBTLE ART OF SYNCHRONIZATION

SO, YOU'VE MASTERED the art of the sideways glance (or at least, you're working on it). You've perfected the "accidental" brush of the hand (okay, maybe it wasn't so accidental). You've even navigated the treacherous waters of small talk without completely imploding. But there's a secret weapon in the arsenal of attraction, a subtle art that can elevate your interactions from polite pleasantries to genuine connection: mirroring and matching.

Think of it as the ultimate social chameleon act, but without the creepy factor. Mirroring and matching isn't about becoming a carbon copy of the person you're with; it's about subtly aligning your nonverbal cues with theirs, creating a sense of harmony and unspoken understanding. It's like a silent conversation happening beneath the surface of your words, a nonverbal tango of connection.

Imagine this: you're chatting with someone, and they subtly lean forward, their eyes widening as they recount a particularly exciting anecdote. Without even realizing it, you find yourself mirroring their posture, leaning in slightly, your own eyes reflecting their enthusiasm. This isn't conscious mimicry; it's an unconscious response, a natural inclination to synchronize with someone we find engaging. It's the body language equivalent of saying, "I'm listening, I understand, and I'm on your wavelength."

The power of mirroring lies in its subtleness. You're not overtly copying their every move—that would be bizarre and likely send them running for the hills. Instead, it's about picking up on their key nonverbal cues—their posture, their gestures, their pace of speech—and subtly aligning your own behavior accordingly. It's about creating a sense of rapport, a feeling of shared rhythm and understanding.

Think of it like this: you're at a concert, and everyone is swaying to the music. You might not consciously decide to sway, but you find yourself naturally joining in the collective movement. Mirroring and matching in social interactions work on a similar principle—a subconscious synchronization that creates a feeling of connection and ease.

Let's break it down:

- **Posture:** If they're leaning back, relaxed and open, you might subtly mirror that relaxed posture. If they're leaning forward, engaged and interested, you can subtly reflect that energy. However, avoid blatant imitation. If they're slouching dramatically, don't suddenly collapse into a heap beside them. Subtly adjust your posture to match the overall feeling of their body language—open and engaging versus closed off and reserved.

- **Gestures:** This is where things get interesting. Do they use expansive gestures when they talk, or are their movements more contained? Match the energy level of their gestures. If they're using lots of hand movements, feel free to incorporate some of your own, but avoid becoming a hyperactive gesticulator. The key is congruence, not a carbon copy.

- **Pace of Speech:** Are they speaking rapidly, excitedly, or are they more deliberate and measured? Adjust your pace to match theirs. If they're speaking quickly, don't suddenly slow down to a snail's pace. The goal is to create a natural flow of conversation, not a jarring mismatch.

- **Facial Expressions:** This is perhaps the most subtle and important aspect of mirroring. Do they smile often? Do their eyebrows raise in surprise? Subtly mirror their facial expressions to show that you're actively engaged and empathetic. A shared smile is a powerful tool of connection, but a forced or exaggerated smile will fall flat.

Now, let's address the elephant in the room (or, more accurately, the slightly awkward mime in the corner): What if your mirroring attempts backfire? Well, it's a risk. Sometimes, people might pick up on what you're doing, and some might find it slightly unsettling. That's why subtlety is key. Remember, you're not trying to become a puppet, just to create a sense of shared energy.

Think of it as a well-orchestrated dance. You're not leading or following strictly; you're responding, adapting, and creating a harmonious rhythm. The goal isn't to perfectly synchronize, but to create a feeling of shared understanding and connection.

Consider the context, too. Mirroring someone who's clearly stressed and agitated wouldn't be appropriate; you might inadvertently amplify their negative feelings. Use your judgment and intuition. Mirroring is a tool, not a robotic command.

Another important point to remember is that mirroring is most effective when it's genuine. If you're trying to force it, it will likely come across as unnatural and even creepy. Let it flow naturally from your genuine interest and engagement with the other person. Focus on actively listening, being present, and connecting with them on a human level.

Let's look at some examples where mirroring might work wonders, and equally, where it would be disastrous:

Scenario 1: The Coffee Shop Encounter

You're at your favorite coffee shop, and you notice someone who catches your eye. They're reading a book, occasionally sipping their latte, a slight smile playing on their lips. They seem relaxed and engaged in their own world. As you approach, you might subtly mirror their relaxed posture, perhaps leaning back against the counter yourself. You can then engage them by asking about their book or making a lighthearted comment about the coffee. The subtle mirroring helps to create an atmosphere of ease and comfort, making it easier to strike up a conversation.

Scenario 2: The Networking Event

You're at a networking event, and you're trying to make a connection with someone in your field. They're actively engaged in a conversation, their body language open and expressive. As you approach, you might subtly mirror their energy level, adopting a similar posture and using similar hand gestures. This helps to create a sense of connection and common ground, making it easier to join their conversation and build rapport.

Scenario 3: The Disaster Zone—Avoid these

You're on a first date, and your date is clearly uncomfortable. They keep fidgeting, avoiding eye contact, and their body language is closed off. Mirroring their nervous energy would only amplify the awkwardness.

Instead, focus on creating a relaxed and comfortable environment. You could subtly adjust your posture to be more open and inviting, hoping to encourage them to do the same. Forced mirroring here would be a recipe for a disastrous date.

Mirroring is a tool, not a guaranteed path to instant attraction. It works best in conjunction with genuine interest, active listening, and a genuine desire to connect with another person. It's about creating a harmonious interaction, a nonverbal symphony of understanding, where both parties feel comfortable and engaged.

It's not a magic bullet—it won't make someone fall madly in love with you if they're not interested to begin with—but it can certainly make your interactions smoother, more engaging, and hopefully, more successful in fostering genuine connections. So, go forth and subtly synchronize. Just remember to keep it subtle, keep it genuine, and be prepared for the occasional, hilarious slip-up. After all, even the most skilled social chameleons have their off days.

SHARED INTERESTS AND COMMON GROUND
FINDING YOUR TRIBE

SO, YOU'VE SUBTLY mirrored your way into a conversation, maybe even landed a laugh or two. Congratulations! You've navigated the initial hurdles. But let's be honest, a shared giggle over a clumsy waiter doesn't exactly equate to a lifelong bond. That's where the real magic (or at least, the significantly less awkward magic) comes in: shared interests and common ground.

Think of it like this: you're building a house. Mirroring and matching is laying the foundation—crucial, yes, but not exactly the most aesthetically pleasing part. Shared interests are the beautiful, intricately designed rooms, the cozy fireplace, the stunning view from the window. They're what you'll actually live in. Without them, you've got a structurally sound but ultimately empty shell. A house that will probably attract some pretty awkward houseguests, metaphorically speaking.

Finding common ground isn't about finding someone who's your exact clone. That would be incredibly boring, and frankly, a bit terrifying. It's about discovering those connecting threads, those shared passions that weave a tapestry of connection. It's about finding your tribe. And yes, that sounds cheesy, but bear with me. Because finding your tribe is far less cheesy than ending up alone, watching reruns of "Friends" while eating ice cream directly from the tub. We've all been there. (Don't judge.)

So how do you unearth these shared interests and, crucially, how do you avoid accidentally revealing your alarming collection of vintage rubber ducks? (Some things are best kept secret, even from your tribe.)

The most obvious approach is simply talking to people. I know, revolutionary, right? But instead of the usual small talk about the weather (which, let's be honest, is rarely a compelling conversation starter unless you're a meteorologist or a particularly enthusiastic cloud-gazer), try asking open-ended questions that reveal more about their passions and hobbies. Instead of "How's the weather?", try, "What are you passionate about these days?" or "What's something you're really excited about?"

This simple shift in questioning can unlock a treasure trove of information. Are they obsessed with competitive ferret-legging? Fantastic! (Okay, maybe not fantastic for everyone, but you get the point.) Do they spend their weekends restoring vintage cars? Excellent! Do they knit tiny sweaters for squirrels? Admirable! (Though, maybe tread carefully on the squirrel knitting front; some lines shouldn't be crossed.)

The key is to genuinely listen to their responses. Don't just wait for your turn to talk about your own impressive collection of vintage rubber ducks (again, resist the urge). Truly listen, ask follow-up questions, and show a genuine interest in what they have to say. Remember, people love talking about themselves—it's a fundamental human need. Give them the space to do so, and you'll build a far more substantial connection than you would by dominating the conversation with tales of your rubber duck dynasty.

Beyond casual conversation, consider exploring shared activities. Joining a club, taking a class, or volunteering are all fantastic ways to meet people who share your interests. Think about your hobbies and passions. Do you love hiking? Join a hiking group. Are you a budding astrophysicist (or just someone who enjoys looking at the stars)? Attend a stargazing event. Are you a fan of competitive cheese rolling? Well, let's hope there's a club for that...

These shared activities provide a natural context for interaction and conversation. You already have something in common—the activity itself—which acts as a built-in icebreaker. It takes the pressure off trying to find common ground from scratch, allowing for more organic connections to form. Plus, you'll be learning something new, meeting new people, and potentially avoiding the awkwardness of a pick-up line gone wrong. It's a win-win situation, even if you're terrible at the activity itself. Nobody's judging your disastrous attempt at pottery. Well, maybe some people are, but most people are too busy focusing on their own disastrous attempt.

Online communities also offer a powerful way to connect with like-minded individuals. Whether it's a forum dedicated to a specific hobby, a social media group centered around a shared interest, or even a dating app that filters users based on their interests, the internet provides a vast network of potential connections. Just remember to be cautious, practice safe internet habits, and avoid sending unsolicited pictures of your rubber ducks. Again, crucial.

However, even with the right tools, finding your tribe isn't always a smooth, effortless process. Sometimes you'll encounter people whose interests align with yours, but the connection just doesn't click. And that's okay. It's not a reflection on you or your worth. It simply means that you haven't found the right fit yet. Finding meaningful connections takes time, patience, and a healthy dose of self-awareness.

Don't be discouraged by setbacks. Keep putting yourself out there, engaging in activities that you enjoy, and focusing on building genuine connections. Remember, the goal is to find people who make you feel good about yourself, who appreciate you for who you are, rubber ducks and all. (But maybe keep the rubber ducks to a minimum on the first few dates.)

And remember, the true measure of success isn't just about the quantity of connections you make, but the quality. A small group of close friends who share your values and passions is far more fulfilling than a vast network of superficial acquaintances. So focus on building those deep, meaningful bonds. It's worth the effort, even if it involves a few awkward encounters along the way. Because let's be honest, the stories you'll tell later will be infinitely more entertaining than any perfectly smooth, predictable interaction. Embrace the chaos, the laughter, the occasional cringe-worthy moment. It's all part of the journey towards finding your tribe—your own quirky, wonderful, and possibly slightly rubber-duck obsessed group of friends.

Finally, a word of caution: be wary of those who seem too eager to embrace your eccentricities. While a genuine appreciation for your collection of vintage rubber ducks is admirable, a too enthusiastic embrace might be a red flag. Sometimes, people are not who they seem. Trust your instincts. If something feels off, it probably is. Your inner detective should always be on high alert, especially when dealing with potential new friends and their potential admiration of your rubber ducks. The stakes are high! Your carefully curated collection's reputation is at risk.

Remember, finding your tribe isn't just about finding people who share your hobbies; it's about finding people who genuinely appreciate you for who you are, quirks, rubber ducks, and all. So go forth, explore, connect, and enjoy the slightly chaotic, wonderfully rewarding journey of building meaningful relationships. And if you happen to meet someone who shares your passion for competitive ferret-legging, well, congratulations! You've struck gold. Just be sure to check their background thoroughly before introducing them to your rubber ducks. You never know who might have a secret vendetta against aquatic fowl.

AUTHENTICITY VS. ARTIFICE BEING YOURSELF AND WHY IT MATTERS

LET'S FACE IT, the dating world (and the world of making friends, for that matter) is a minefield of carefully constructed personas. We're all walking around with our carefully curated Instagram feeds in our heads, desperately trying to project an image of effortless cool, witty banter, and a life overflowing with exciting adventures (even if those adventures mainly involve meticulously arranging succulents and perfecting the art of the avocado toast). But here's the truth: authenticity trumps artifice every single time. Think of it as the ultimate dating hack—one that requires zero cheesy pickup lines and a minimum of awkward silences.

The problem with artifice is that it's exhausting. Imagine trying to maintain a false front—the "I-spontaneously-speak-fluent-Mandarin-

and-climb-Mount-Everest-on-weekends" facade—for any extended period. It's like wearing a pair of shoes two sizes too small; initially, you might manage a wobbly walk, but eventually, your feet will start screaming in protest. And so will your soul. The strain of pretending to be someone you are not palpable, a constant low-level anxiety that permeates every interaction. It's like trying to build a house on a foundation of lies; sooner or later, the whole thing will come crashing down.

Authenticity, on the other hand, is liberating. It's about embracing your quirks, your imperfections, and yes, even your slightly embarrassing obsessions with vintage thimbles or competitive cheese rolling. When you're genuinely yourself, the interactions become effortless, genuine, and infinitely more rewarding. Think of it as the "comfortable shoes" approach to social interaction: you might not be strutting down the runway, but you're comfortable, you're confident, and you can actually walk without the fear of tripping over your own carefully constructed lie.

Now, I'm not suggesting you walk around broadcasting every single embarrassing detail of your life. That's not authenticity; that's just broadcasting. Authenticity is about being honest in your self-presentation, revealing your true self in a way that feels natural and comfortable for you. It's about letting your genuine personality shine through, imperfections and all. Think of it as a finely crafted piece of pottery—slightly imperfect, perhaps with a unique crack or two, but beautiful in its uniqueness. No two pieces are exactly alike, and that's precisely what makes them special.

The beauty of being authentic is that it attracts the right people. People who appreciate the genuine article, the real you—quirks and all. Imagine spending time with someone who's constantly putting on a show, trying to impress you with fabricated tales of adventure. Exhausted yet? Now imagine spending time with someone who's genuinely themselves—a little quirky, a little awkward, but utterly captivating in their honesty. Who would you prefer to spend time with? The choice, my friends, is quite clearly a no-brainer.

But how do you actually become more authentic? It's not a switch you can flip overnight, but rather a gradual process of self-discovery. It starts with self-awareness—a deep understanding of your strengths, weaknesses, values, and beliefs. Spend some time reflecting on who you are, what makes you tick, and what truly matters to you. Journaling can be a great tool for this kind of introspection, allowing you to unpack your thoughts and feelings without judgment.

Once you've gained a clearer understanding of yourself, the next step is to start expressing that self more openly. This might involve setting boundaries, saying "no" to things that don't align with your values, or simply being more honest in your interactions with others. It's about making choices that are aligned with your true self, even when it's uncomfortable. Remember, it's okay to be vulnerable; in fact, it's often the path to genuine connection.

Authenticity doesn't mean being completely unfiltered and blurting out every thought that pops into your head (unless you happen to be a stand-up comedian, in which case, carry on). It's about being genuine in your interactions, presenting yourself honestly without trying to be someone you're not. It's the difference between saying "I'm having a fantastic day!" when you're actually feeling a bit under the weather and saying, "I'm a bit tired today, but things are going okay." The latter is honest, vulnerable, and ultimately more relatable.

One of the biggest hurdles to authenticity is the fear of judgment. We worry about what others will think if we reveal our true selves, fearing that they won't accept our quirks and imperfections. But this fear is often unfounded. People are far more accepting than we give them credit for. In fact, embracing your unique qualities can make you more attractive, setting you apart from the crowd of perfectly polished, utterly generic individuals. Think of it as adding that special sprinkle of "interesting" to the bland cupcake of conformity.

Let's use an example. Imagine you're passionate about collecting vintage rubber ducks. It's a quirky hobby, perhaps not conventionally "cool," but it's undeniably you. In the past, you might have hidden this passion, fearing ridicule. But now, embracing your authenticity, you mention your collection during a conversation. This seemingly small act can be a powerful way to connect with others. You might surprise yourself by finding others who share your enthusiasm, or even those who are fascinated by your unique interest, viewing it not as strange but as a testament to your individuality.

Furthermore, authenticity fosters deeper connections. When you're being genuine, people feel seen, heard, and understood. There's a profound sense of trust and intimacy that develops when you let your guard down and reveal your true self. These are the foundations upon which strong, meaningful relationships are built. They aren't based on carefully constructed facades, but on genuine appreciation for each other's unique selves. These are the relationships that truly matter—the ones where you don't have to pretend, where you can relax, be yourself, and revel in the shared comfort of being authentically you.

Another aspect to consider is how authenticity influences self-esteem. Constantly striving to maintain a false persona is incredibly draining on your self-worth. It creates a constant internal dissonance, where your outer presentation clashes with your inner reality. This leads to feelings of inadequacy and self-doubt, making it harder to form genuine connections. Conversely, embracing your authentic self fosters self-acceptance and strengthens your self-esteem. When you're comfortable in your own skin, it radiates outwards, making you more confident and approachable. It's the ultimate self-care strategy, and trust me, your inner self (and those vintage rubber ducks) will thank you for it.

So, ditch the carefully crafted masks, the rehearsed lines, and the fabricated narratives. Embrace the wonderful, slightly messy, gloriously imperfect truth of who you are. Authenticity isn't about being perfect; it's about being real. And in a world saturated with artifice, being real is revolutionary. It's a breath of fresh air, a unique flavor in a world of bland conformity. It's the secret weapon in the dating game (and the game of friendship), the key to unlocking deeper, more meaningful connections. So, go forth, be yourself, and watch as the right people are magnetically drawn to your wonderfully authentic glow. Just remember to keep your rubber ducks away from overly enthusiastic dogs. Some things are just too precious to risk.

THE POWER OF VENERABILITY LETTING YOUR GUARD DOWN SLIGHTLY

BUILDING GENUINE CONNECTIONS, whether romantic or platonic, often feels like navigating a treacherous
obstacle course blindfolded. We're taught to present a polished, almost flawless version of ourselves,
carefully concealing our quirks, insecurities, and
occasional existential dread. But what if the key to
unlocking deeper relationships lies not in hiding our
imperfections, but in strategically revealing them?
This isn't about becoming a walking, talking confes-
sional booth, unloading every embarrassing detail of
your life onto unsuspecting strangers. It's about the
art of carefully chosen vulnerability—a delicate dance
between guardedness and openness.

Think of it like this: imagine trying to assemble
IKEA furniture without the instructions. You could
spend hours wrestling with oddly shaped pieces,

muttering obscenities under your breath, and ending up with a wobbly monstrosity that vaguely resembles a bookshelf. Or, you could admit you're completely flummoxed and ask for help. The latter approach, while potentially humiliating in the short-term, ultimately leads to a functional bookshelf and, possibly, a new friend (or significant other) who's impressed by your willingness to admit when you need assistance. That's the power of vulnerability in action.

Now, before you start envisioning yourself weeping uncontrollably at the first sign of social interaction, let's clarify: carefully chosen vulnerability is not about oversharing or seeking sympathy. It's about selectively revealing aspects of your authentic self that build trust and create connection. It's about showing a crack in the armor, not a gaping hole in your emotional defenses. It's the difference between casually mentioning your embarrassing childhood incident with a pet hamster and recounting every traumatic experience from your past with graphic detail. Subtlety is key. Remember, we're aiming for "intriguing" not "terrifying."

One effective way to introduce vulnerability is through self-deprecating humor. It's a surprisingly powerful tool for building rapport, demonstrating self-awareness, and even making yourself appear more approachable. Imagine this scenario: You're at a party, awkwardly clutching a lukewarm glass of something bubbly. You could approach someone with a rehearsed line like, "So, what do you do?" Or, you could try something like, "I'm terribly out of my element here. I usually only socialize with my cat, and even he's judging my choice of footwear tonight." The self-deprecating approach instantly humanizes you, creating an opening for connection based on shared awkwardness and a hint of endearing vulnerability.

The key here is to avoid self-deprecation that borders on self-loathing. The goal isn't to beat yourself up, but to demonstrate self-awareness with a touch of humor. It's about owning your flaws without dwelling on them. This is a crucial distinction. There's a difference between saying, "I'm a hopeless klutz and I tripped over the rug five minutes ago," and saying, "I'm such a failure; I tripped over the rug and am convinced my life is a series of catastrophic missteps." The first is charmingly awkward; the second is emotionally draining.

Remember the adage, "People are drawn to authenticity"? Well, authenticity includes acknowledging our imperfections. It's not about pretending to be someone else but about embracing the wonderfully flawed human being you already are. Sharing a small imperfection—a silly habit, a quirky obsession, or a past mistake—can surprisingly build connection. This isn't about revealing your deepest, darkest secrets on a first date; it's about letting your guard down just a little, creating space for genuine connection.

Consider the power of storytelling. Sharing a personal anecdote, even a mildly embarrassing one, can be a powerful way to build rapport. It shows you're comfortable being yourself and reveals something about your personality and values. Just make sure your stories are relevant to the conversation and not just random life ramblings. Nobody wants to hear the full, gory detail of your unfortunate incident involving a rogue squirrel and a plate of meticulously crafted mini-quiches. We're aiming for relatable, not traumatizing.

Vulnerability also involves being open to rejection. It takes courage to put yourself out there, to risk being vulnerable. You might not always get the response you're hoping for, and that's okay. Rejection is a part of life; a humbling experience that teaches us resilience and helps us refine our approach. Don't let the fear of rejection paralyze you; embrace it as a learning opportunity. Each rejection is a step closer to finding a connection that resonates. Moreover, remember that not every connection is meant to be a long-term, life-altering relationship. Some interactions serve the valuable purpose of providing learning and growth, even if they don't lead to a deep friendship or romance.

This doesn't mean launching into a detailed confession of your deepest insecurities on first meeting someone. That would likely be met with a polite, but swift, exit. Think of vulnerability as a slow reveal, a gradual unfolding of your true self, layer by layer, as trust is established. Start with small, safe disclosures, and observe the other person's reaction. Their response will be a valuable guide in determining how much you're comfortable sharing. Pay attention to non-verbal cues, like body language and tone of voice. If they seem uncomfortable or disengaged, it might be time to dial it back.

Furthermore, remember the context. Vulnerability is not a one-size-fits-all strategy. What works in one situation may not work in another. Sharing your deepest fear of clowns with a potential romantic partner on a first date might not be the best icebreaker, whereas a casual mention of your love for badly drawn cats might create a memorable and endearing moment. The key is to use your judgment and choose your moment wisely.

In short, the art of carefully chosen vulnerability is about striking a balance between self-protection and genuine connection. It's about being authentic, yet mindful. It's about showing your human side without overexposing yourself. It's the fine art of letting your guard down—slightly. It's a skill that takes practice, patience, and a healthy dose of self-awareness, but the reward is the potential for deeper, more meaningful connections than you could ever achieve by hiding behind a carefully constructed facade. So, breathe in, breathe out, and take a small, courageous step toward unveiling the wonderfully imperfect, utterly unique you. The right people will be wait-ing. Just remember to keep the rubber ducks far, far away from those overly enthusiastic dogs—trust me on this one.

CHAPTER 4
AVOIDING THE
DATING APOCALYPSE

COMMON PITFALLS AND HOW TO
AVOID THEM

THE GHOSTING GAME
DEALING WITH DISAPPEARING ACTS

AH, GHOSTING. The digital equivalent of being abducted by aliens, only instead of probing, you're left with the lingering question: "Did I do something?" The answer, more often than not, is a resounding "Probably not, but who knows in the grand scheme of cosmic dating?"

Ghosting isn't just about disappearing from someone's phone; it's a full-blown performance art of emotional abandonment. Think of it as a silent, dramatic exit, complete with a slow fade-out, leaving the ghosted party desperately searching for answers, much like a detective in a poorly written noir film. They're left sifting through the digital breadcrumbs, analyzing every text, every emoji, every fleeting moment of perceived connection, only to find nothing but digital dust. The only clue? A deafening silence.

The psychology behind ghosting is as fascinating

as it is frustrating. Some ghosters are cowards, lacking the courage to have an uncomfortable conversation. They'd rather vanish into the digital ether than face the awkwardness of a direct rejection. Others are simply emotionally unavailable, incapable of handling the complexities of a genuine human interaction. They prefer the fleeting, low-commitment nature of online interactions, avoiding the responsibility of a real relationship. Still others might be masters of the "soft ghost," slowly reducing contact, responding less frequently, and eventually fading away—the equivalent of a slow, agonizing death by a thousand paper cuts.

Then there's the "benching" phenomenon, where someone keeps you dangling on the hook, just close enough to give you hope but never truly committed. They're the players of the dating game, keeping you on the sidelines as their backup option, while pursuing other prospects. It's like being a contestant on a reality show, except the prize is a slightly less painful rejection.

So, how does one navigate this minefield of digital disappearances? The first step, and perhaps the most difficult, is accepting that ghosting isn't a reflection of your worth. It's a reflection of the ghoster's immaturity, emotional unavailability, or sheer cowardice. You're not doing anything wrong; they're simply incapable of handling adult relationships, preferring the escapism of the digital world.

Think of it this way: would you want someone

who lacks the courage to express their feelings directly? Someone who values silence over communication? Someone who treats you like a disposable item? Probably not. Ghosting, therefore, is a self-selecting process; it weeds out those who aren't worth your time and energy. Consider it a fortunate escape from a potential relationship disaster.

Once you've processed the initial sting of rejection (allow yourself a healthy dose of Ben & Jerry's and a trash-talking session with your friends), it's time to focus on self-care. Remember that your self-worth is not defined by someone else's inability to communicate. Engage in activities that nourish your soul: read a good book, binge-watch a captivating series, or finally learn that ukulele you've been eyeing.

It's also important to avoid the temptation to analyze every detail, every "maybe" or "perhaps." Overthinking only prolongs the pain and reinforces the ghoster's power. Let go of the need to understand their actions. Their reasons are their own, and often quite frankly, irrelevant to your well-being.

However, the lack of closure is one of the most frustrating aspects of ghosting. It leaves you wondering: "What could I have done differently?" The truth is, often very little. Ghosting is almost always about the ghoster, not the ghosted. It's a reflection of their inability to communicate, not your shortcomings.

But, if you are inclined to self-reflection (and who isn't occasionally?), consider these points: Were your communication style clear and consistent? Did you respect their boundaries? Did you give them space when needed? Reviewing these aspects can help you refine your approach in future interactions, but remember to focus on improving your own communication, not trying to "fix" someone else's behavior.

Moving forward, it's essential to set healthy boundaries. Don't invest too much time and emotional energy into someone you've only interacted with online. Maintain multiple connections, avoid putting all your eggs in one basket. Remember the dating world is diverse and offers many possibilities; don't let one ghostly encounter discourage you.

And, most importantly, remember to laugh. The absurdity of ghosting, the sheer audacity of someone vanishing into thin air, is almost comical. Find the humor in it, because let's face it, it's a ridiculous behavior. Laugh at the absurdity, not at yourself. You deserve better than to be treated like a ghost. You deserve someone who values open communication, honesty, and the courage to have a face-to-face (or at least a text-to-text) conversation.

So, the next time you find yourself ghosted, remember this: you dodged a bullet. You avoided a relationship with someone who lacks the emotional maturity and communication skills for a healthy connection. It might sting, it might be confusing, but ultimately, it's a win. Consider it a cosmic intervention, diverting you from a potentially disastrous relationship, guiding you towards someone who appreciates you for who you truly are, flaws and all. And that, my friend, is worth celebrating. Now go get yourself some ice cream. You've earned it.

Let's also address the slightly less dramatic, but equally frustrating, phenomenon of the slow fade. This isn't a sudden disappearance, but a gradual tapering off of communication. It's like watching a plant slowly wilt, a slow, agonizing death by neglect. The texts become less frequent, the calls less enthusiastic, and eventually, silence reigns supreme. This is the emotional equivalent of being slowly strangled by a particularly passive-aggressive cactus.

The slow fade, while less jarring than ghosting, is often even more confusing and emotionally draining. You're left questioning every interaction, every seemingly innocuous remark, searching for clues in the dwindling communication. It's a game of emotional detective work, and you're the only one playing.

Dealing with a slow fade requires similar coping mechanisms as with ghosting: self-care, avoiding overthinking, and focusing on your own well-being. The key difference lies in the potential for a little more clarity. While a ghoster leaves no trace, a slow fader might offer some subtle hints, some breadcrumbs of explanation. These clues, however minuscule, can help you process the situation, and perhaps provide a (slightly) less painful exit. But if the clues are confusing and the process is overly prolonged, don't hesitate to walk away from the slowly withering plant. You deserve a garden full of blooming relationships, not a dying cactus.

Furthermore, let's not forget the "breadcrumbing" variation. This involves receiving intermittent, sporadic communication, just enough to keep your hopes up, but not enough to constitute a genuine connection. These digital crumbs are just enough to keep you hooked, ensuring your continued attention and emotional availability while the sender keeps their options open. It's a cruel game of emotional yo-yo, leaving you perpetually dangling between hope and despair. In the case of breadcrumbing, self-preservation is key. Recognize the pattern and understand that this behavior is indicative of an unhealthy dynamic that doesn't serve you in the long run. Cut off contact and spare yourself the endless cycle of emotional ups and downs.

Ultimately, ghosting and its variations are reflections of the ghoster's emotional immaturity and inability to communicate effectively. It says far more about them than about you. While the experience is undeniably painful and frustrating, it provides a valuable opportunity for self-reflection and growth. Learn from the experience, focus on your well-being, and remember that you deserve better than a disappearing act. You deserve a relationship built on open communication, mutual respect, and genuine connection. Now, go forth and conquer the dating world, one hilarious anecdote at a time.

THE FRIEND ZONE
NAVIGATING PLATONIC
BOUNDARIES

SO, YOU'VE DODGED the ghosting bullet, navigated the minefield of flaky daters, and somehow managed to avoid spontaneously combusting from sheer dating-app-induced anxiety. Congratulations! You're officially a dating ninja... or at least, a survivor. But the trials of the modern romantic landscape don't end there. We now enter the treacherous territory of the Friend Zone, a place where hopes and dreams go to die a slow, agonizing death, often accompanied by the faint scent of awkward silences and shared Netflix binges.

The Friend Zone is a peculiar phenomenon. It's a purgatory of platonic affection, a land where romantic aspirations are subtly (or sometimes brutally) rejected, leaving the hopeful romantic stranded in a wasteland of "just friends." The tricky part is that the boundaries can be remarkably blurry. One minute, you're sharing inside jokes and late-night philosophical debates over questionable pizza; the next, you're questioning whether that lingering touch on the arm was accidental or a desperate plea for rescue from the depths of unrequited love.

The key to navigating this delicate landscape is discerning genuine platonic connection from a situation that's teetering on the edge of romantic potential, but is ultimately headed for heartbreak (or at least a substantial amount of internal existential crisis). Let's be honest, sometimes the signs are glaring, like a neon sign screaming "NOT INTERESTED!" Other times, they're as subtle as the difference between a genuine smile and a polite grimace. And that, my friend, is where the real challenge lies.

One common pitfall is the "over-investment" syndrome. This is where you pour your heart and soul (and perhaps a bit too much time and effort) into a friendship, hoping that sheer devotion will magically transform it into a romance. Picture this: You're constantly available for spontaneous coffee dates, readily offer emotional support, even go as far as to help them move a ridiculously heavy bookshelf (that they totally could have done on their own). Meanwhile, they're content with the arrangement, happy to receive all that love and support without reciprocating romantic interest. This is often a recipe for disaster. The more you invest, the greater the potential for disappointment.

Another subtle trap is the "misinterpretation of kindness." This is where friendly gestures are mistaken for romantic signals. They might have a warm, engaging personality, but this doesn't automatically translate to romantic interest. Let's say someone always laughs at your jokes. That's great! But it doesn't mean they're secretly pining for you. Likewise, offering thoughtful advice, or remembering details about their lives, these are acts of friendship, not necessarily declarations of love. The distinction is crucial, and often missed. This leads to the painful realization that your interpretation of their actions was entirely your own.

So, how do you navigate this perilous path without completely losing your mind (or your dignity)? The answer lies in careful observation and, dare I say it, clear communication. Firstly, observe their behavior. Do they actively seek out time with you alone, or is it mostly group settings? Do they initiate contact, or are you usually the one reaching out? Do they engage in physical touch that goes beyond friendly gestures? These subtle cues, though not foolproof, can offer valuable insight.

Secondly, consider their words. Do they ever mention dating other people? Do they express romantic interest in other individuals? This isn't about being paranoid; it's about being realistic. If they're openly talking about dating other people, it's a pretty strong indicator that they're not interested in you romantically.

Thirdly, and this is the most important point: communication. The fear of rejection often leads us to avoid difficult conversations. But sometimes, a direct (yet tactful) conversation is the only way to get clarity. This doesn't have to be a dramatic, tear-filled confrontation. It can be as simple as casually mentioning your feelings and observing their reaction. However, before you do, assess your confidence in the situation. If you feel it's a completely lost cause, then letting go might be the most sensible and least painful option.

Let's say you've observed the subtle cues, listened carefully to their words, and you're still uncertain. Consider a subtle test. Try casually mentioning a date you're going on with someone else. Observe their reaction. Genuine friends will be happy for you. Someone harboring secret romantic feelings might show some (subtle, hopefully) signs of jealousy or disappointment. Again, be mindful; this isn't about manipulating their emotions, but about gently gathering information.

However, even with all the careful observation and subtle tests, there is a chance you still end up in the dreaded friend zone. The harsh reality is that sometimes, someone just isn't romantically interested, and that's okay. It doesn't diminish your worth or attractiveness. It simply means you weren't the right match for that particular person. It's essential to accept this gracefully, and to not turn into a bitter, resentful version of yourself. Maintaining a friendship while accepting that there is no romantic interest is also a valuable skill—a true sign of emotional maturity!

Consider the alternative scenario: you've navigated the friend zone and it becomes clear that the interest is reciprocated. Congratulations! But don't dive headfirst into a relationship without carefully considering the dynamics. The foundations of a successful relationship are built on trust and mutual respect. A shift from friendship to romance requires mutual consent and a careful transition. Be clear about expectations and communicate open and honestly. Don't assume that because you've transitioned from friends to lovers, communication should be any less important. This is probably the most important advice for any relationship.

The Friend Zone, like most things in the dating world, is a complex beast. It's a mix of misinterpretations, missed signals, and a healthy dose of wishful thinking. But by understanding the common pitfalls, developing keen observational skills, and practicing open communication, you can navigate this tricky terrain and avoid the heartache (and potentially awkward Thanksgiving dinners). Remember, it's a journey, not a race, and the occasional stumble is part of the experience. So, equip yourself with knowledge, a sense of humor, and a healthy dose of self-respect, and venture forth into the romantic wilds with confidence. You got this! And if all else fails, there's always the comfort of the platonic friendship, complete with endless movie nights and questionable pizza choices. At least you'll have a great friend, right?

And for those who truly revel in the Friend Zone, perhaps it's time to re-evaluate your strategies. Are you inadvertently sending out mixed signals? Are you unconsciously setting yourself up for disappointment? This isn't about blame; it's about honest self-assessment. Consider adjusting your approach: perhaps communicate your intentions more clearly, setting boundaries and expectations. If you're genuinely interested in a romantic connection, then platonic relationships won't suffice. Being a great friend is a fantastic quality but should not be a substitute for a romantic partnership. And if it still doesn't work out, remember that some relationships are meant to stay platonic. You are worthy of a romantic connection that is fulfilling, happy and satisfying; this doesn't mean that platonic relationships aren't also valuable.

Furthermore, remember that the dynamics of friendships and romantic relationships can be significantly different. Friendships often thrive on shared interests and activities. Romantic relationships are more deeply rooted in emotional intimacy and often require a level of vulnerability that friendships may not necessarily necessitate. Understanding the distinctions between these types of relationships can help you clarify your own emotional needs and expectations, preventing potential disappointment and misinterpretations down the line. Are you seeking someone to share deep emotional connection with, or are you primarily seeking companionship? Knowing this will significantly help you navigate romantic relationships and maintain healthy platonic friendships.

It is also crucial to note that the pursuit of a romantic relationship should never come at the expense of a genuine friendship. If you find that your romantic desires are causing significant strain or damage to your friendship, it's a clear sign that perhaps it's time to re-evaluate your actions and priorities. Respecting boundaries and recognizing that not every friendship is destined for romance is crucial. Ultimately, healthy relationships, whether romantic or platonic, are built on mutual respect, open communication, and a genuine appreciation for the other person. Focusing on cultivating these aspects can ensure you have a fulfilling connection, regardless of whether it's romantic or platonic. The quest for love should not come at the cost of your friendship.

So, there you have it: a deep dive into the intriguing, often frustrating, and sometimes hilarious world of the Friend Zone. Remember, navigating the complexities of human connection is a lifelong journey, filled with triumphs, setbacks, and plenty of opportunities for self-discovery. So embrace the awkward moments, learn from your experiences, and remember to always laugh along the way—especially at yourself. Because let's face it, the dating world is absurd, and sometimes, the best we can do is to laugh in the face of it all. And if you do end up firmly planted in the Friend Zone, at least you have a friend. Right? Hopefully one who doesn't require you to move their exceptionally heavy bookshelf single-handedly.

THE OVERSHARE TRAP
MANAGING INFORMATION
OVERLOAD

WE'VE CONQUERED the Friend Zone, dodged the ghosting gremlins, and survived the dating app apocalypse's initial onslaught. You're a seasoned veteran, a dating warrior, possibly even sporting a metaphorical medal of honor fashioned from discarded dating profiles. But before you raise a celebratory mimosa (or lukewarm tap water, let's be honest, dating can be expensive), there's one more treacherous terrain to navigate: the Overshare Trap. This isn't about accidentally revealing your undying love for pineapple on pizza (although, that's a whole other conversation). This is about the art—or rather, the science—of controlled information disclosure. Think of it as the fine art of strategic revelation, carefully unveiling aspects of your personality like a master chef plating a Michelin-star meal, rather than dumping the entire contents of your fridge onto a plate in one chaotic, unappetizing heap.

Because let's face it, we've all been there. That first date, butterflies fluttering like trapped moths in your stomach, and suddenly, you're spilling your entire life story—childhood traumas, regrettable fashion choices of yesteryear, the embarrassing incident involving a karaoke machine and a poorly chosen rendition of "Bohemian Rhapsody." Before you know it, you've laid bare your soul, your deepest insecurities, and the fact that you still have a collection of Beanie Babies stashed under your bed (don't judge, they're collectors' items now!). This, my friend, is the Overshare Trap, and it's a sticky one.

The human brain, that wonderfully chaotic organ, is a master of pattern recognition. It craves order, predictability, and a healthy dose of mystery. Bombarding a new acquaintance with a torrent of personal information before they've even had a chance to figure out if they like the color of your socks is a surefire recipe for disaster. Think of it like this: you wouldn't walk into a job interview and immediately launch into a detailed account of your most embarrassing bathroom accident, would you? (Unless, of course, the job is a stand-up comedian. In that case, go for it!)

Oversharing is like serving up an entire banquet before your guest has even tasted the amuse-bouche. It overwhelms, it exhausts, and it can leave a lingering feeling of discomfort, like the time you accidentally wore mismatched shoes to a wedding. The person on the receiving end might feel pressured, overwhelmed, and frankly, a little creeped out. Remember, mystery is an aphrodisiac. A little intrigue goes a long way. Revealing too much too soon can be the equivalent of showing someone the ending of a movie before they've even seen the opening credits. It spoils the experience.

So, how do we avoid this potentially dating-apocalypse-inducing pitfall? The key is gradual, strategic disclosure. Think of it as a slow reveal, like a suspenseful TV drama. Start with the basics: your name, your profession (or at least a vague description that doesn't involve detailing your daily struggles with a malfunctioning coffee machine), and your general interests. Avoid sensitive topics like past relationships, family drama, or your deep-seated fear of clowns (unless clowns are your thing, in which case, more power to you!).

Let the conversation flow naturally. Allow the other person to reciprocate, to share their own information at their own pace. This is a dance, not a race. If they ask about your childhood, you don't have to launch into a full-blown biographical saga, complete with sound effects. A concise, carefully curated anecdote will suffice. Think of it like a well-crafted cocktail—a few key ingredients, expertly mixed, leaving the recipient wanting more. Don't dump the entire bottle of vodka into the glass at once!

Let's explore some common oversharing scenarios and how to navigate them with grace and a healthy dose of self-awareness. Imagine this: you're on a date, the conversation is flowing smoothly, and then, BAM! You suddenly confess your deep-seated fear of pigeons. While not necessarily a deal-breaker, it's a detail best saved for a few dates down the line, when a certain level of trust and comfort has been established.

Instead of blurting out your irrational aversion to feathered city dwellers, try a gentler approach. Perhaps a lighter, more humorous anecdote involving a particularly aggressive pigeon. This allows you to hint at your phobia without overwhelming your date with the full spectrum of your avifauna-related anxieties. The goal is to create intrigue, not to send them running for the hills.

Another classic oversharing pitfall involves your exes. Oh, the exes! The landmines of past relationships, waiting to explode at the slightest provocation. Unless your date specifically asks about your dating history (and even then, tread carefully), it's best to steer clear of this potentially explosive topic. Nobody wants to hear a blow-by-blow account of your previous romantic escapades, especially on a first date. A simple, "I'm focusing on myself and enjoying the present moment," will suffice. Remember, less is more, especially when it comes to discussing your dating past.

Similarly, avoid unsolicited details about your finances, your family drama (we all have it, but not everyone wants to hear about yours), and your deeply personal medical history. These are private matters that should be handled with discretion and shared only when the time is right and a level of trust has been established.

And finally, a word about social media. Your carefully curated Instagram feed might seem like an open invitation to overshare, but think again. While it's tempting to share everything, remember that social media is a highlight reel, not a documentary of your life. It's okay to keep some aspects of your personality and life private, to maintain a certain level of mystery and intrigue.

Mastering the art of controlled information disclosure is a journey, not a destination. It takes practice, self-awareness, and a healthy dose of humor. Don't be afraid to make mistakes—we all do. The important thing is to learn from them, to adjust your approach, and to remember that mystery is a powerful tool in the dating game. It's like a delicious culinary experience: you don't want to reveal all the ingredients at once, you want to leave your date craving more. So, embrace the slow reveal, savor the suspense, and watch your dating life blossom—one carefully chosen detail at a time. And remember, if all else fails, you can always blame it on the pigeons. They're always a good scapegoat.

THE EXPECTATION GAME
MANAGING UNREALISTIC IDEALS

SO, YOU'VE NAVIGATED the treacherous waters of the Overshare Trap, emerged victorious (or at least, still breathing), and are ready to tackle the next hurdle in this exhilarating, often absurd, journey we call dating. Let's talk about expectations. Specifically, the wildly unrealistic, often fantastical, sometimes downright delusional expectations we tend to slap onto potential romantic partners. This, my friends, is the Expectation Game, and it's a game rigged against you unless you learn to play it smart.

We've all been there, haven't we? Scrolling through dating profiles, crafting a mental image of the perfect person: the impossibly handsome/beautiful, witty, financially secure, emotionally available, adventurous, kind, understanding, perfectly-coiffed individual who shares your exact passion for obscure 80s synth-pop and artisanal cheese. This person, of course, doesn't exist. Or, if they do, they're probably already married to a unicorn and living in a cloud made of cotton candy.

The problem isn't dreaming big; the problem is mistaking those dreams for reality. We build up these unrealistic ideals based on idealized portrayals in movies, TV shows, and the carefully curated highlight reels that are social media profiles. Suddenly, everyone seems to be living a charmed life, filled with exotic vacations, perfect relationships, and enough avocado toast to feed a small village. It's a cruel illusion, a digital mirage designed to make you feel inadequate. And that, my friends, is a recipe for dating disaster.

The truth is, real people are messy. They have flaws. They have bad hair days (sometimes weeks!). They might snore like a freight train, hoard socks, or have a questionable taste in music. And that's okay! That's normal! Embracing imperfection, both in others and ourselves, is the cornerstone of a healthy relationship. Expecting someone to be flawlessly perfect is like expecting a perfectly round orange; it simply doesn't exist in nature.

One of the biggest culprits in the Expectation Game is the "Prince/Princess Charming" syndrome. We carry around this idealized vision of a perfect partner who will magically solve all our problems, fulfill all our desires, and make us instantly happy. Newsflash: relationships are a two-way street, a collaborative effort, not a magical cure-all for all that ails you. Expecting someone else to fix your emotional baggage is not only unfair, it's a recipe for disappointment.

Consider this: Are your expectations based on genuine compatibility and shared values, or are they fueled by a desperate need to fill a void within yourself? Honest introspection is crucial. If you're constantly searching for someone to "complete" you, you're setting yourself up for a fall. A healthy relationship is a partnership between two whole individuals, not two halves desperately trying to become one.

Another common pitfall is the "comparison trap." We tend to compare our romantic lives (or lack thereof) to those around us, fueled by the curated perfection of social media. We see photos of couples on idyllic vacations and think, "Why don't I have that?" This comparison game is not only unfair but utterly unproductive. Everyone's journey is unique; there's no standardized timeline for love, happiness, or anything else for that matter. Remember that Instagram is a highlight reel, not a documentary.

So, how do we escape the clutches of the Expectation Game? How do we set realistic expectations without becoming cynics resigned to a life of solitude and questionable TV dinners?

First, acknowledge your unrealistic expectations. Be honest with yourself. What are the unrealistic standards you've set for your ideal partner? Write them down. Analyze them critically. Do they stem from societal pressure, past experiences, or a healthy dose of unrealistic romantic comedies? Once you've identified the culprits, you can begin to dismantle them.

Secondly, focus on self-improvement. The more secure and confident you are in yourself, the less likely you are to project unrealistic expectations onto others. Work on your self-esteem, nurture your passions, cultivate your own happiness. When you're already content in your own life, you'll be less likely to cling to a partner to fill a void within you.

Third, be mindful of your dating profile and how it might be contributing to unrealistic expectations. Don't present a flawless version of yourself. Showcase your personality quirks, interests, and even your flaws. Honesty attracts authenticity, which leads to healthier relationships in the long run.

Fourth, practice mindful communication. Open and honest communication is key to any successful relationship. Don't bottle up your expectations, but don't launch them like a grenade, either. Express your desires and needs respectfully, and be open to compromise.

Fifth, embrace imperfection. Remember those flaws we talked about? Embrace them in yourself and others. It's what makes us unique and interesting. Authenticity beats perfection every time.

Finally, don't be afraid to walk away from a relationship that isn't meeting your needs, even if it seems to tick all the "perfect" boxes on paper. Sometimes, the relationship that looks perfect on the outside is suffocating on the inside. Trust your gut.

The Expectation Game is a tough one, I won't lie. It requires self-awareness, honest reflection, and a hefty dose of self-compassion. But remember, the goal isn't to find perfection; it's to find someone compatible, someone who values you for who you are, flaws and all. It's about finding a connection based on mutual respect, shared interests, and a willingness to navigate life's ups and downs together—even if those downs involve questionable sock choices and questionable karaoke performances. So, ditch the impossible standards, embrace the reality of messy humans, and get ready to play the dating game with a healthy dose of self-awareness and a whole lot of humor. Because let's be honest, if you can't laugh at the absurdity of it all, what's the point? Besides, laughter is a pretty good icebreaker. Just don't start with a joke about the dating apocalypse. That's been done to death. Unless you can come up with a truly original one. In that case, I'm listening. And maybe, just maybe, I'll even share it with my readers. You never know, it might become the next dating app catchphrase. Just remember to give me co-credit. And a small percentage of your potential future profits. It's only fair, after all, I helped you get there. Just kidding (mostly). Now go forth and date! But be realistic, please. My therapist is very expensive.

COMMUNICATIONS BREAKDOWN THE ART OF EFFECTIVE COMMUNICATIONS

HAVING SUCCESSFULLY NAVIGATED the treacherous waters of unrealistic expectations (and hopefully, emerged with your sanity intact), we now arrive at a crucial juncture in our dating expedition: communication. Or, more accurately, the often-hilarious, sometimes excruciating, frequently baffling lack of communication that can torpedo even the most promising romantic prospects faster than a poorly timed joke at a family reunion.

Think of communication as the scaffolding of any relationship. Without it, the whole thing is liable to collapse into a heap of misunderstandings, unmet needs, and simmering resentment—the perfect recipe for a dating apocalypse. We've all been there, haven't we? That sinking feeling when you realize you've been talking at someone, not with them, resulting in a communication chasm wider than the Grand Canyon.

The problem isn't always about what we say; it's often about what we don't say, what we imply, what we assume. We're masters of subtext, aren't we? We build elaborate castles of unspoken desires and expectations, then get utterly bewildered when our romantic counterparts fail to decipher our cryptic messages. It's like sending a love letter written entirely in hieroglyphics and expecting a passionate reply. The chances of success? Slim to none. Unless, of course, your date happens to be an Egyptologist with a penchant for romance. In that case, congratulations! You've found your soulmate—and a fascinating conversation starter.

Effective communication is about clarity, honesty, and a willingness to listen. It's about articulating your needs and desires without resorting to mind-reading (a skill, I assure you, is not taught in any reputable dating manual). It's about being vulnerable enough to share your feelings, even the messy, uncomfortable ones, without fear of judgment. And yes, it involves actively listening to your date, not just waiting for your turn to speak. We all have that one friend (or are that one friend) who expertly steers conversations back to themselves, a feat of conversational judo that leaves their date feeling like a forgotten potted plant. Avoid this at all costs!

Let's delve into some common communication

pitfalls and how to avoid them. First up, the dreaded "Passive-Aggressive Poke." This involves expressing your discontent through subtle, often indirect means. Leaving passive-aggressive notes, using sarcasm as your primary mode of communication, or giving the silent treatment are all classic examples. Think of it as a communication landmine—carefully concealed, capable of inflicting significant emotional damage, and guaranteed to escalate conflict rather than resolve it.

Why do we resort to passive-aggression? Because direct communication can feel terrifying. It requires courage, honesty, and a willingness to confront potential conflict. It's easier to sulk, send a cryptic text, or hope our partner magically intuits our unspoken frustrations. But trust me, this approach is a recipe for disaster. It creates confusion, fosters resentment, and leaves everyone feeling unheard and misunderstood.

Instead of the passive-aggressive poke, opt for the "Direct and Honest Jab." It's less elegant, perhaps less subtle, but far more effective. Say what you mean, clearly and directly. Use "I" statements to express your feelings without blaming your date. For example, instead of saying, "You never listen to me!", try, "I feel unheard when our conversations are dominated by one person; it would be helpful if we could share the floor time equally." See the difference? One is an accusation, the other is a constructive request.

Next on our list of communication calamities: The

"Assumption Avalanche." We assume our date shares our values, our desires, our interpretations of events. We build elaborate narratives based on limited information, creating a perfect storm of misunderstandings. Let's say your date cancels a date without offering a clear reason. Do you assume they're not interested? Or are they dealing with a family emergency? Always verify your assumptions; don't rely on speculation alone. It is just asking for trouble.

The solution? Ask clarifying questions. Communicate your need for more information. Don't jump to conclusions, especially if there is no apparent cause for assumption. Active listening involves more than just hearing words; it involves interpreting emotions, understanding body language, and asking for clarification when needed.

Then there's the "Communication Blackout," the radio silence that descends after a disagreement, creating a chilling vacuum of emotional unavailability. This avoidance strategy might seem like a way to escape conflict, but it's a surefire method for creating further misunderstandings. If you've had a disagreement, don't retreat into your shell; talk it out! Finding a way to approach a misunderstanding to find a solution is always better than silence.

Instead of ignoring your partner, practice the art of "Constructive Conflict Resolution." This involves calmly discussing your disagreements, acknowledging each other's viewpoints, and actively searching for a compromise. It may not be the easiest path, but it's definitely the most rewarding one. Think of it like a negotiation, not a war. The goal isn't to "win" the argument; it's to find a solution that works for both of you.

Finally, let's talk about the dreaded "Mixed Signal Medley." This involves sending conflicting messages, leaving your date utterly confused and, frankly, exhausted. You say one thing but do another. You express interest but then disappear for days. This inconsistency creates uncertainty, anxiety, and ultimately, mistrust. It's akin to setting up a dating obstacle course with invisible walls and random booby traps—guaranteed to trip up even the most experienced daters.

The antidote? Be clear and consistent in your words and actions. If you're interested in someone, let them know. If you're not, let them know. Avoid playing games or sending confusing signals. Honesty, while sometimes painful, is always the most respectful approach in the long run.

Effective communication isn't about being perfect; it's about being willing to communicate honestly, openly and respectfully. It's about being mindful of your words and actions, understanding that miscommunications are inevitable, but also resolving to learn from them. It's about listening as much as you speak. It's about building a relationship based on mutual understanding, not on assumptions and cryptic messages.

So, embrace the challenge. Practice the art of effective communication, even if it feels awkward or uncomfortable at times. The reward? A stronger, healthier, and far more satisfying dating experience. And maybe, just maybe, you'll avoid the dating apocalypse. But if not, at least you'll have some hilarious stories to tell. Because even amidst the dating chaos, there's always humor to be found, provided you have the communication skills to laugh about it together, rather than wallow in mutual misunderstandings. And isn't that what relationships are really all about? Finding someone who can laugh at your dating disasters alongside you? Because let's face it, we all need someone to share the cringe with. And if that person shares your love of a well-placed pun, then you are on the road to a relationship that truly communicates effectively. Now go forth and communicate! But remember to choose your words carefully. Your future happiness, and possibly your future therapist's bank account, depends on it.

CHAPTER 5
MASTERING THE ART
OF THE FOLLOW-UP

KEEPING THE
CONVERSATION ALIVE

THE SUBTITLE ART OF THE FOLLOW-UP TEXT, TIMING AND TONE

AH, THE FOLLOW-UP TEXT. That precarious dance between eager beaver and creepy stalker. It's a minefield, my friends, a digital expanse littered with the wreckage of unanswered messages and the ghosts of hopes dashed against the cold, hard reality of "seen" but not replied to. But fear not, intrepid conversationalists! We're going to navigate this treacherous terrain together, emerging victorious, armed with the knowledge (and humor) to conquer the art of the follow-up.

Let's start with the elephant in the room (or rather, the tiny, slightly pixelated elephant on your phone screen): timing. There's no magic number here, no universally agreed-upon interval between messages that guarantees success. Think of it like Goldilocks and the Three Bears, but instead of porridge, we have waiting periods. Too short, and you risk appearing desperate, like a lovesick puppy glued to the door, tail a-thumping. Too long, and you risk fading into the abyss of forgotten contacts, becoming just another notification lost in the digital shuffle. The perfect amount of time? It's the one that feels right, a delicate balance calibrated to the unique rhythm of your budding connection.

Consider the context. Did you have a whirlwind conversation fueled by shared laughter and witty repartee? A shorter interval might be appropriate. Did you exchange a polite, but brief, greeting? A longer wait might be in order. Think of it as pacing yourself in a marathon, not sprinting a 100-meter dash. You're building something here, not trying to rush the process. Remember, patience, young Padawan. Patience.

Now, let's talk tone. This is where the nuances of human interaction truly come into play. You're not just sending words; you're conveying emotions, intentions, and personality. A simple "Hey, how was your day?" can be drastically different depending on your delivery. A casual, friendly tone suggests ease and relaxed interest. An overly effusive, exclamation-point-laden message might come across as manic and a bit intense (think: a caffeinated squirrel on a sugar rush). On the other hand, a tone that's too formal or reserved can sound stiff and distant, like communicating with a particularly polite robot.

The key here is authenticity. Let your personality shine through. Don't try to be someone you're not in an attempt to impress. If you're naturally witty, let your humor flow. If you're more reserved, a simple and thoughtful message is perfectly fine. Authenticity beats artifice every single time. Fake enthusiasm can be smelled a mile away (or at least, a mile away on the internet).

Let's look at some scenarios, shall we? Imagine you met someone at a coffee shop, and you exchanged numbers. You could send a follow-up text the next day, something like, "Hey! It was great chatting with you yesterday. That [mention something specific you talked about] was hilarious/interesting/fascinating." This is specific, demonstrates you were paying attention, and keeps the conversation flowing naturally. Avoid generic messages like "Hey, what's up?" It's as exciting as watching paint dry (unless you're into ASMR painting videos, then, go for it).

But what if the response is slow in coming, or worse, nonexistent? Don't spiral into a pit of despair! Give it some time, a day or two, depending on your initial interaction. A second follow-up, if you feel it's appropriate, could be something low-key, like, "Just checking in! Hope you're having a good week." This keeps the door open without being pushy. More than two follow-up attempts, however, might be considered excessive. Sometimes, it's best to accept that the connection might not be there. Move on! The world is full of other fascinating humans, I assure you.

Let's explore the darker arts of follow-up failures.

134

We've all been there: the dreaded "seen" notification, the silent treatment, the slow fade. These digital ghostings are a modern plague, leaving us wondering what we did wrong, whether our pickup line was too cheesy, or our jokes too lame. The truth is, sometimes, there's no good answer. People are complex and have lives outside of our texting interactions.

One thing to avoid: the desperate barrage of texts. This is a surefire way to scare someone off. A flurry of messages, each increasingly more pleading, is a recipe for disaster. Remember that person has a life outside of responding to your messages. It's unlikely to turn a "seen" into an "engaged".

Let's discuss the art of the apology in the context of follow-up communication. Sometimes, despite your best intentions, things can go wrong. Maybe you sent a text that came across differently than you intended. A sincere apology can go a long way in repairing a fractured connection. Keep it brief, genuine, and specific. Avoid making excuses; take responsibility for your actions or words. A simple "Hey, I'm so sorry if my last text came off wrong. I didn't mean to [explain what you didn't mean to do]." can do wonders. However, don't over-apologize, turning a simple misstep into a drawn-out saga.

Rejection, that unavoidable part of the social dance, deserves its own section in this chapter. It's painful, sure, but it's also a learning experience. Instead of dwelling on why things didn't work out, try to view it as feedback. Did you miss any cues? Was the timing off? These are valuable lessons that can help you refine your approach in future interactions. Remember, not every connection is meant to be, and that's perfectly okay.

Let's consider the power of suggestion in follow-up texts. Instead of directly asking for a date, consider subtly suggesting activities. "I saw [Movie Title] is out, have you seen it yet?" or "There's a new exhibit at [Museum Name] that sounds interesting. I've always been into [Topic Related to Exhibit]". This is a less pressured way of suggesting a next step, keeping the ball in their court without demanding a yes or no response.

And finally, the most crucial element in the art of the follow-up text is to be yourself. Don't try to be someone you're not, trying to conform to an image you think someone wants. Embrace your quirks and let your personality shine. A genuine connection is built on authenticity, not artifice.

Beyond the text, there are countless ways to keep a conversation alive. Suggesting a phone call, a coffee date, or a fun activity can take your connection to the next level. The key is to show interest and initiative, but without being overly pushy.

Remember, the goal of a follow-up isn't just to continue the conversation; it's to build a genuine connection. It's about finding common ground, showing empathy and understanding, and ultimately, letting your personality shine through. It's a process, not a race. Enjoy the journey, and don't be afraid to laugh at the occasional stumble along the way. After all, a little awkwardness is just the spice of life, the seasoning of a successful social interaction. Now go forth and conquer those follow-up texts!

BEYOND THE TEXT
PLANNING YOUR NEXT MOVE

SO, YOU'VE MASTERED the art of the initial contact—congratulations! You've successfully navigated the treacherous waters of the first message, dodged the bullet of the dreaded "seen" zone, and even managed a witty response or two. But now comes the real test: keeping the conversation alive. This isn't about relentless texting; it's about building genuine connection through clever engagement, strategic planning, and a dash of delightful unpredictability. Think of it less as a sprint and more as a charming, slightly awkward waltz.

Forget the robotic back-and-forth of "How was your day?" and "It was good, how was yours?" We're aiming for something more engaging, something that sparks laughter, curiosity, and a desire to learn more about the other person—and vice versa. This requires going beyond the simple text exchange and employing some creative, unconventional strategies.

One potent technique is the art of the "unexpected question." Forget the predictable inquiries. Instead, try something like, "If you could have any super-power, but it had to be utterly useless, what would it be and why?" The goal is not to stump them with a brain teaser, but to encourage a playful, imaginative response. It reveals personality quirks and opens avenues for funny, unexpected tangents. Imagine the possibilities: the person who chooses the power to instantly know the nutritional content of any food, only to find themselves analyzing every single bite of their meal with agonizing detail, or the one who can communicate with squirrels, only to discover their conversations are dominated by acorn-based debates.

Another approach is to subtly introduce elements of surprise. Perhaps you mention an unusual hobby, a bizarre childhood memory, or a completely random fact that you find fascinating. This doesn't have to be a blatant attempt to impress; it's about being genuine and revealing aspects of your personality that might not immediately emerge in typical conversation. The key is to keep it light, playful, and relatable. For instance, instead of saying, "I had a great day," you could say, "I just spent an hour trying to teach my cat to play fetch. Let's just say, he's more of a 'stare intensely at the laser pointer' kind of guy." This invites a response, opens the door for shared experiences (pet-related disasters are a universal language, you know?), and adds a touch of humor to the exchange.

Planning beyond the immediate text exchange is crucial. Think about suggesting activities that build on shared interests, or even just something that breaks the monotony of digital communication. Have you both expressed a love for a particular band? Suggest going to a concert together, or at least sharing YouTube videos of their best live performances. This transition from text to something more tangible shows initiative and a genuine desire to build a connection beyond the digital realm. The key here is to keep the suggestions low-pressure and flexible. Frame them as possibilities, not demands. For example, instead of saying, "We should totally go to that concert next week," try, "Hey, I was thinking about that [band] concert next week. It looks fun; would you be interested in checking it out?" This allows them to express their level of interest without feeling obligated.

Remember, the goal is to build a connection, not to orchestrate a meticulously planned social conquest. Be spontaneous, be playful, and most importantly, be yourself. If the conversation starts to lag, don't panic. A well-timed, thoughtful question can breathe new life into even the most stagnant exchange. If you're finding it challenging to keep things going, reflect on what you've learned about their interests during the conversation. Use that knowledge to delve deeper and ask thoughtful questions. For example, if you discovered a shared love for vintage sci-fi movies, instead of saying "Cool!", you could say, "What's your favorite classic sci-fi flick, and why?" The "why" is key here, it encourages a more substantial response than a simple name.

And let's be honest, sometimes conversations just fizzle out. This doesn't necessarily mean you've failed. Sometimes, the chemistry just isn't there, and that's perfectly okay. Don't beat yourself up over it; view it as an opportunity to learn, adjust, and keep practicing. The more you experiment with different strategies, the better you'll become at understanding what works best for you and, importantly, what resonates with other people.

The transition from digital communication to real-world interaction can be particularly tricky. You've cultivated a connection through texting, but now you need to maintain that momentum face-to-face. The key here is to maintain the playful, engaging style that has worked so well in your text exchanges. Don't suddenly become a different person when you meet in person.

One common mistake people make is overthinking the "first date." This is nothing more than an extension of your already-established connection; it's just moving the conversation into the physical realm. It's the next step in building rapport and getting to know each other better. To prepare for this next stage, use the information you've gleaned from your initial conversations to plan activities that you both will enjoy.

Let's say your conversations have revealed a shared love for hiking. A hike, in this case, is a far more effective first date than a stuffy dinner at a formal restaurant. Think about the conversation you'll have while walking side-by-side, surrounded by nature. The relaxed setting encourages casual conversation. You have something in common to talk about, reducing pressure and allowing for more genuine interaction. This is far more effective at building a bond than an awkward silence punctuated by forced pleasantries over lukewarm wine.

On the other hand, if your conversations reveal a shared love for quirky museums or unusual art installations, those might make for more engaging first-date locations than a generic movie theater. The point is to create opportunities for shared experiences that naturally lead to engaging conversations, strengthening your connection in a far more authentic way.

Remember, the goal isn't necessarily to create a romantic relationship, although that's a possible outcome. This is about building connections, making friends, and expanding your social circle. Each interaction, each conversation, is a step towards becoming more comfortable and confident in your social interactions.

Beyond that, consider the long game. Maintaining friendships and connections takes effort and conscious planning. Regular check-ins, thoughtful gestures, and mutual support are key elements in nurturing any relationship, be it romantic, platonic, or professional. Remember those awkward moments during the initial conversations? Those can serve as great fodder for future shared laughter.

Think about it; these "failures" are actually opportunities for connection. Sharing your embarrassing moments, laughing about the times things went wrong, are powerful bonding experiences. They humanize you, making you more relatable and approachable.

Don't be afraid to express genuine interest and curiosity. People appreciate being listened to, truly listened to. Show genuine interest in their lives, their aspirations, their challenges. The art of a successful follow-up isn't about perfect phrasing or flawless delivery; it's about being authentic, engaging, and consistently showing that you care. And who knows, along the way you might find yourself laughing harder and connecting deeper than you ever thought possible. So go forth, armed with wit, charm, and a healthy dose of self-awareness, and conquer the art of the follow-up. The world (and your social circle) awaits!

MAINTAINING MOMENTUM
KEEPING THE CONNECTION STRONG

SO, YOU'VE SUCCESSFULLY navigated the perilous initial contact, dodged the digital ghosting bullet, and even managed to elicit a chuckle or two. Fantastic! But the journey of connection is far from over. Think of the first contact as merely setting the stage for a grand, slightly awkward, possibly hilarious performance. Maintaining momentum—that's where the real artistry lies. It's not about bombarding your new acquaintance with endless messages; it's about the delicate dance of engagement, a carefully choreographed tango between wit and genuine interest.

The key to keeping the connection strong lies in understanding that you're not just exchanging words, you're building a bridge. And bridges, my friends, need more than just a few hastily thrown-together planks. They require sturdy foundations, a well-thought-out design, and perhaps a little bit of artistic flair. Let's build that bridge, one carefully crafted message at a time.

First, let's address the pachyderm in the room—the dreaded "over-messaging" pitfall. We've all been there, haven't we? That moment when the witty banter morphs into a relentless barrage of texts, each one slightly less amusing than the last, leaving your recipient scrambling for an escape route faster than you can type "LOL." Avoid this fate by embracing the art of strategic silence. Think of it as a calculated pause, a moment for the other person to process, to respond, to perhaps even miss you a little (yes, a little healthy missing is good!). Give them space to breathe, to live their lives outside the confines of your increasingly frantic messages. Let the conversation ebb and flow naturally, rather than forcing it into a relentless, exhausting sprint.

Variety is the spice of life, and the same applies to your digital interactions. Avoid the monotonous back-and-forth of predictable questions and answers. Instead, sprinkle in some delightful unpredictability. Share a funny anecdote, send a quirky meme that reminds you of them (but make sure it's actually relevant!), or suggest a fun, low-pressure activity. Perhaps a virtual game of "two truths and a lie," a shared playlist of songs that encapsulate your current mood, or even a playful challenge. This keeps the conversation fresh, exciting, and prevents it from becoming stale and predictable.

Remember that genuine connection hinges on genuine interest. This isn't about pretending to be someone you're not; it's about actively listening and showing that you're truly invested in the other person. Ask open-ended questions that go beyond superficial pleasantries. Instead of "What do you do?", try "What's something you're passionate about right now?" This encourages them to share their passions, their dreams, their quirks. And listen attentively! Don't just wait for your turn to speak; actively engage with what they're saying, asking follow-up questions that demonstrate genuine curiosity. People crave connection, and nothing fosters it quite like feeling truly heard and understood.

Let's talk about the power of shared experiences. In the digital age, it's easy to feel disconnected, but sharing experiences—even virtual ones—can strengthen your bond. Suggest watching a movie or TV show together (Netflix Party, anyone?), listening to a podcast simultaneously, or playing an online game. These shared experiences create a sense of camaraderie and shared laughter, fostering a stronger connection than just exchanging text messages ever could.

Now, let's tackle the tricky terrain of scheduling a face-to-face meeting. This is where the rubber meets the road, where the digital connection transforms into something tangible and real. But don't pressure your new acquaintance into a meeting before they're ready. Gauge their interest, their comfort level, and their schedule. Suggest a low-pressure, casual setting, such as grabbing coffee or attending a local event. The goal is to transition from the digital realm to the real world smoothly, without creating unnecessary anxiety or pressure.

Finally, remember the importance of self-awareness. Not every connection will blossom into a lifelong friendship or romance. Some conversations will fizzle out, and that's okay. Don't take it personally. It's a numbers game, a process of trial and error. Learn from each interaction, refining your approach, and honing your ability to connect with others.

Maintaining momentum isn't about manipulation or gamesmanship; it's about building genuine rapport, fostering mutual interest, and creating a space for connection to flourish. It's about appreciating the subtle art of the digital dance, understanding the rhythms of communication, and responding to the cues of your newfound acquaintance. It's a journey of exploration, discovery, and maybe, just maybe, the beginning of a beautiful, albeit slightly awkward, friendship. So, go forth, armed with wit, genuine interest, and a healthy dose of patience, and conquer the art of maintaining momentum. The world of meaningful connections awaits!

And remember, even the most perfectly crafted message can fall flat if it lands at the wrong time. Consider their schedule, their lifestyle, and their potential availability. Sending a witty message at 3 am might be received as enthusiastic, but more likely as a slightly creepy intrusion. Time your messages strategically, showing you are considerate of their time and routine.

The art of the follow-up isn't just about maintaining the conversation; it's about cultivating a connection. It's about creating a sense of anticipation, intrigue, and shared excitement. It's about building a relationship brick by brick, message by message, laugh by laugh. Think of it as building a Jenga tower, carefully placing each message to support the next, always mindful of the precarious balance. One wrong move, one insensitive comment, and the whole thing could come crashing down.

Remember, the aim is to build a genuine connection, not just a string of witty exchanges. Genuine interest is crucial, and it shines through in the questions you ask, the stories you share, and the active listening you demonstrate. People are drawn to authenticity. Don't try to be someone you're not; embrace your quirks, your humor, and your unique perspective. The right people will appreciate the real you.

But let's face it, sometimes even the most genuine and well-intentioned efforts can fall flat. Not every conversation is destined to become a friendship. Sometimes, the connection simply isn't there, and that's okay. Don't take it personally; it's part of the process. Learn from every interaction, identify what worked and what didn't, and adjust your approach accordingly. Consider it a valuable learning experience in the grand, often hilarious, tapestry of human interaction.

The art of the follow-up is a journey, not a destination. It's a continuous process of learning, adapting, and refining your approach to connection. It's about embracing the unpredictability, navigating the awkward silences, and finding the humor in the unexpected turns. It's a testament to the resilience of the human spirit and our inherent need to connect, to share, and to laugh along the way.

So, keep those conversations alive, nurture those connections, and remember to embrace the wonderfully chaotic, often hilarious, journey of human interaction. The rewards, in terms of friendship, camaraderie, and maybe even a little romance, are well worth the effort. Just remember to breathe, to be yourself, and to have fun along the way. After all, life's too short to take the art of connection too seriously. Embrace the awkwardness, the laughter, and the potential for meaningful connection. The world, and your social circle, are waiting.

THE ART OF APOLOGIES
REPAIRING RELATIONSHIP RIFTS

LET'S FACE IT, even the most charming conversationalist—and I use that term loosely, considering my own track record—occasionally steps in a conversational landmine. We've all been there. That moment when your perfectly crafted witty remark backfires spectacularly, landing somewhere between unintentionally offensive and downright hilarious. Or, perhaps, you accidentally stepped on someone's emotional toes, leaving a trail of awkward silence in your wake. This isn't about avoiding conflict entirely (because let's be honest, that's about as realistic as finding a unicorn riding a unicycle at a poetry slam). It's about mastering the graceful art of the apology, the social equivalent of a well-executed ninja move. Think of it as damage control, but with significantly more humor.

The key to a successful apology isn't just about uttering the words "I'm sorry," although that's a good starting point. It's about understanding why you need to apologize, and crafting an apology that's both genuine and effective. It's about showing, not just telling. Imagine this: you've just told a joke that bombed harder than a souffle in a hurricane. Instead of shifting uncomfortably and muttering about the "terrible acoustics," own it. "Okay, that was a clanger," you can admit, a self-deprecating grin spreading across your face. "My comedic timing clearly needs some work, or perhaps I need a new career." Self-awareness is your secret weapon here; the ability to laugh at yourself diffuses tension and shows you're not taking yourself too seriously.

But what about those times when the faux pas goes beyond a failed joke? Let's say you unintentionally made a comment that was insensitive or hurtful. This requires a more nuanced approach. Generic apologies—"I'm sorry if I offended you"—often fall flat. They lack sincerity and come across as defensive. Instead, try to pinpoint the specific action or statement that caused the offense. For example, instead of the generic apology, you could say, "I'm truly sorry for saying [specific comment]. I didn't realize it would come across as [how it was perceived], and I understand why you're upset. I was insensitive, and I regret it." See the difference? Specificity demonstrates genuine remorse and a willingness to understand the other person's perspective.

Another important element of a successful apology

is empathy. Put yourself in the other person's shoes. Try to understand how your actions made them feel. Acknowledging their feelings—even if you don't fully agree with their interpretation of events—validates their experience and shows you care. For example, "I understand that my comment about [topic] made you feel [their emotion], and I deeply regret causing you that pain." Notice how this approach focuses on their feelings rather than justifying your actions. It's about making them feel heard and understood, which is far more powerful than any simple "sorry."

The timing of your apology is also crucial. Don't let days, or worse, weeks go by before addressing the situation. The longer you wait, the more the offense festers, creating a chasm of misunderstanding that's harder to bridge. A timely apology shows that you value the relationship and that you're not trying to sweep the incident under the rug. Remember that sometimes a quick, heartfelt apology on the spot can be more effective than a grand, overly-thought-out one later.

And here's where things get interesting. Sometimes, an apology isn't enough. It's not a magic eraser that instantly removes all traces of conflict. It's more like a first step on a path towards reconciliation. Depending on the severity of the offense, the other person might need time to process their emotions. Respect that. Don't bombard them with follow-up messages, expecting immediate forgiveness. Give them space to cool off, reflect, and decide how to move forward.

However, don't assume silence equates to rejection. If the situation warrants it, a thoughtful follow-up a day or two later can be beneficial. This isn't about nagging; it's about demonstrating your continued concern. It could be a simple, "Just wanted to check in and see how you're doing. I hope you're feeling better." This shows you're still thinking about the situation and the other person's well-being. Avoid making excuses or trying to minimize your actions in this follow-up. Instead, reaffirm your sincerity and willingness to make amends.

Beyond the words themselves, your body language and tone play a significant role in conveying sincerity. A mumbled, insincere apology delivered while checking your phone is about as effective as using a feather to extinguish a bonfire. Maintain eye contact, speak calmly and clearly, and show genuine remorse through your facial expressions. Your body language should reflect the sentiment of your words. If your words say "I'm sorry," but your body screams "I don't really care," your apology will fall flat.

Furthermore, consider the context of the apology. A public apology might be necessary for more serious offenses, while a private conversation might suffice for smaller misunderstandings. The setting should align with the gravity of the situation. A grand, public spectacle of an apology for accidentally spilling someone's drink is overkill, while a whispered apology in the corner for a more serious offense might feel dismissive. Consider the audience and choose your setting wisely.

The art of the apology is a skill that develops over time. It involves self-awareness, empathy, and a willingness to take responsibility for your actions. It's not always easy, and it might feel awkward at times, but the ability to apologize effectively can save relationships, mend broken trust, and even create a deeper connection with others. It shows maturity, humility, and a commitment to making things right. And who doesn't want to cultivate those qualities? Besides, a genuine apology can be surprisingly cathartic, even if the initial situation was less than stellar.

Consider the alternative: harboring resentment and allowing a minor misunderstanding to fester into a major rift. That's a recipe for social disaster. The art of a well-delivered apology is like a well-placed piece of duct tape—it repairs the damage, mends the tears and prevents further unraveling. It's a skill that will serve you well, not only in your relationships but also in your personal growth. So, practice those apologies, embrace the awkwardness, and watch your social skills soar (or at least prevent a complete social implosion).

Finally, remember that forgiveness isn't always immediate. Sometimes, the person you offended needs time to process their emotions before they can truly forgive you. Respect their timeline and avoid pressuring them. Keep your communication open and sincere, but allow them the space to heal. A genuine apology paves the way for reconciliation, but it doesn't guarantee instant forgiveness. It's a process, not a quick fix. Just as we've navigated the complexities of initial contact, let's remember that the path to repairing relationships is equally multifaceted. Embrace the process and try to learn from your mistakes. And, if all else fails, remember, you can always blame the dog. Or the cat. Or the faulty WIFI connection. Seriously, it's amazing how many problems that can solve. Just kidding (mostly).

REJECTION RESILIENCE
BOUNCING BACK FROM REJECTION

SO, YOU'VE BRAVELY ventured forth, armed with your wit (or at least, your best attempt at wit), and you've initiated contact. You've navigated the treacherous waters of small talk, perhaps even managed a genuine laugh or two. And then... silence. Not the comfortable, companionable silence of shared understanding, but the deafening, soul-crushing silence of rejection. The digital equivalent of a slammed door in your face, except this door is made of pixels and stings just as much.

Let's be honest, rejection stings. It's the social equivalent of getting a wedgie in slow motion, while everyone around you watches and pretends not to notice. It's a universal experience, regardless of your charm level (or lack thereof). Even the most charismatic among us have faced the cold shoulder, the unreturned text, the ghosting so complete it makes Houdini look like an amateur.

The key isn't to avoid rejection entirely—that's about as likely as finding a perfectly symmetrical avocado toast—but to develop a thick skin, a resilience to the inevitable bumps in the road of social interaction. It's about bouncing back, not breaking.

Think of rejection as a form of feedback, albeit a rather blunt and sometimes cryptic one. It's not a personal attack, necessarily. It's more like the universe subtly (or not-so-subtly) suggesting you might want to adjust your approach. Maybe your opening line was a bit...much. Or perhaps your timing was off. Maybe you accidentally started a debate on the merits of pineapple on pizza when a simple "hello" would have sufficed. Whatever the reason, the important thing is to learn from it and move on.

One of the worst things you can do after rejection is to overanalyze it to the point of mental exhaustion. We're masters of creating narratives, often negative ones. Suddenly, you're analyzing every word, every gesture, every perceived slight, creating a dramatic internal monologue that would make Shakespeare blush. You start to question your entire being, your worth as a human being, your choice of socks that day. This spiral of self-doubt is a dangerous rabbit hole.

So how do we avoid this descent into self-flagellation? Distraction is your friend. Engage in activities that make you feel good—exercise, hobbies, spending time with supportive friends and family.

Don't let rejection define your day, or your week, or even your month. Remember that one person's "no" doesn't mean a universal "never."

Another crucial component of resilience is the art of self-compassion. Be kind to yourself. Treat yourself as you would treat a dear friend who's just experienced a similar setback. Would you berate your friend? Probably not. So, apply the same level of understanding and empathy to yourself.

Remember the time you spent hours crafting the perfect email, only to receive an automated response that said, "Thank you for your interest. We'll be in touch"? Or the time you put on your best outfit, only to have someone ignore you completely? It happened, and yet, the world kept spinning, the sun still rose, and you managed to function, probably even managed a good laugh about it later. Rejection is a temporary setback, not a life sentence.

Furthermore, perspective is key. Consider the sheer number of interactions you've had in your life. The countless people you've met, some you've connected with, others...not so much. Rejection is just a small blip on the radar of your life's grand adventure. It's part of the process, the inevitable ebb and flow of social interaction.

Let's talk about the elephant in the room: the dreaded ghosting. This digital disappearance act is a modern phenomenon, as baffling as it is painful. Someone you were connecting with simply vanishes, leaving you with unanswered texts and a lingering sense of confusion and rejection.

The truth is, ghosting is often less about you and more about the other person. Their reasons for disappearing might range from being overwhelmed, feeling unsure, or even dealing with personal issues they're not ready to share. Whatever the reason, it's rarely a reflection of your worth as a person. It's important to resist the temptation to personalize ghosting and turn it into a referendum on your character.

A healthy response to ghosting is to acknowledge the situation, feel the sting of rejection, and then... let it go. It's easier said than done, but dwelling on it is a recipe for unhappiness. Focus your energy on yourself and the people who appreciate and value you.

Now, let's talk about analyzing those rejections—without spiraling into self-doubt. Rejection is like a cryptic crossword puzzle. You don't have all the answers, but you can make some educated guesses. Did you come on too strong? Was the timing off? Did you accidentally mention your extensive collection of vintage rubber ducks? (It's a niche interest; I understand.) These are valuable clues, not indictments of your character.

This analytical process, however, shouldn't be a 24/7 occupation. Set aside some time to reflect, make notes (mental or otherwise), and then move on. Otherwise, you risk turning your life into a perpetual replay of every rejection, an endless loop of self-criticism. You're not a detective solving a complex case; you're simply navigating the sometimes-bumpy terrain of human interaction.

Furthermore, cultivate a sense of humor about it all. Rejection can be awkward, painful, even humiliating, but there's often a darkly comedic aspect to it. Think back on some of the most embarrassing moments of your life. Chances are, you can now laugh about them. The same will be true for many rejections. Humor is a powerful tool for coping with difficult emotions. It helps you distance yourself from the pain and see the situation with more perspective.

Finally, remember that resilience isn't a static trait; it's a muscle you can strengthen. Every time you bounce back from rejection, you become stronger and more confident. Each experience is a lesson, an opportunity to grow and refine your approach. It's about learning from your mistakes, not letting them define you.

So, the next time you face rejection, remember this: It's not the end of the world. It's a minor detour on the road to finding genuine connection. It's a chance to learn, grow, and maybe even have a good laugh at your own expense along the way. After all, life's too short to take rejection too seriously—unless, of course, it's from your favorite bakery about their chocolate croissants. That's a different level of heartbreak entirely.

CHAPTER 6
THE LONG GAME

BUILDING MEANINGFUL
CONNECTIONS

BEYOND THE FIRST DATE CULTIVATION LONG TERM RELATIONSHIPS

SO, YOU'VE NAVIGATED the treacherous waters of the first date. Congratulations! You've survived the awkward silences, the potentially disastrous food choices (was that a rogue piece of broccoli stuck in your teeth the entire time?), and the agonizing post-date text-message purgatory. But hold onto your hats, because the real adventure begins now. We've talked about the initial spark, the witty banter (or lack thereof), and the art of the follow-up. But building a meaningful, long-term connection requires more than just a well-timed compliment and a charming smile. Think of it as leveling up in the game of life—you've conquered the first boss, but the final battle is still a long way off.

Let's face it, the first date is like a carefully orchestrated audition. You're both putting on your

162

best performance, showcasing your wit, charm, and (hopefully) impeccable table manners. The pressure is on! But once the initial excitement fades, the real work begins. This isn't about maintaining a meticulously crafted facade; this is about authentic connection, vulnerability, and the messy, beautiful reality of human interaction. It's about peeling back the layers of carefully constructed personas and discovering the genuine person beneath.

Think of it like this: the first date is the appetizer, a tantalizing glimpse of what might be. The long-term relationship is the main course—a slow-cooked masterpiece that requires patience, seasoning (lots of communication!), and a willingness to share the occasional burnt dish (because, let's be honest, everyone messes up sometimes).

One of the biggest misconceptions about long-term relationships is that they require constant fireworks. While those initial sparks are exhilarating, they're not sustainable. Think of it like a roller coaster—the initial plunge is thrilling, but you wouldn't want to spend your entire day on that single drop. A successful long-term relationship is more like a scenic train ride, offering a comfortable pace, beautiful views, and plenty of time for meaningful conversation.

So, how do you cultivate this comfortable, scenic ride? It's not about grand gestures or extravagant displays of affection (although those are certainly nice!). It's about the small, consistent acts of kindness, respect, and understanding that build a strong foundation. It's about listening attentively, not just waiting for your turn to speak. It's about offering support during challenging times and celebrating victories, big and small. It's about remembering their favorite coffee order, even when you're both running on three hours of sleep.

Communication is key—and not just the kind where you meticulously craft the perfect text message. This is about honest, open dialogue, even when it's uncomfortable. It's about sharing your vulnerabilities, your fears, and your hopes, without the fear of judgment. Remember that vulnerability isn't weakness; it's a courageous act that fosters intimacy and trust. It allows you to show the real, imperfect you, and that's where true connection thrives. It's about learning to navigate disagreements constructively, finding common ground, and understanding that compromise is not surrender, but a testament to your mutual respect.

This also requires a healthy dose of self-awareness. Before you can build a strong relationship with someone else, you need to build a strong relationship with yourself. Take some time for introspection—what are your strengths and weaknesses? What are your needs and expectations in a relationship? Understanding yourself will help you communicate your needs effectively and avoid falling into unhealthy relationship patterns. It will also allow you to choose partners who are compatible with your values and goals.

Beyond romantic relationships, fostering long-term connections extends to friendships. These are the unsung heroes of our lives, the people who offer unwavering support, share in our laughter and tears, and provide a much-needed sense of belonging. Cultivating strong friendships requires the same principles as romantic relationships—communication, respect, and genuine care. It's about being present, listening actively, and offering support, even when life gets chaotic. Nurturing these friendships isn't just about maintaining existing connections; it's about actively seeking new ones and expanding your social circle. Join clubs, attend events, volunteer—put yourself out there and create opportunities to meet like-minded individuals.

Building a strong social network also contributes to your overall well-being. It provides a support system during difficult times, offering comfort, advice, and a sense of belonging. It can also enrich your life in countless ways, providing opportunities for new experiences, learning, and personal growth. And remember, it's a two-way street—nurturing these connections requires effort and commitment from both sides.

Remember those awkward first encounters we discussed earlier? The ones where you tripped over your words or accidentally spilled coffee on your date? These experiences, as cringe-worthy as they may seem at the time, are opportunities for growth. Learning to laugh at yourself, to embrace imperfections, and to view setbacks as learning experiences is crucial for navigating the complexities of relationships. It's about embracing the journey, celebrating the victories, and learning from the inevitable stumbles along the way.

Think of building meaningful connections as a marathon, not a sprint. It requires patience, perseverance, and a willingness to show up, even when it's challenging. It's a continuous process of growth, learning, and adapting. It's about embracing the beautiful messiness of human interaction and appreciating the unique and wonderful individuals who enrich our lives. So, go forth, my friends, and build those meaningful connections—one slightly awkward conversation, one heartfelt laugh, one shared cup of coffee at a time. And remember, even if you stumble along the way, the journey itself is an adventure worth taking. The true reward lies not in the destination, but in the beautiful, often hilarious, journey of building meaningful connections. Now, go forth and conquer (or at least, don't spill your coffee).

FRIENDSHIP FIRST
THE POWER OF PLATONIC
CONNECTIONS

WE'VE CONQUERED the initial hurdles of romantic connections, navigating the minefield of first dates and the subsequent agonizing wait for a text. But let's be honest, the romantic ideal often portrayed in movies and sitcoms is...well, a bit of a fantasy. Real-life relationships, even the successful ones, require a lot more than just sparks and stolen glances. They need solid foundations, and surprisingly, those foundations are often built not on romance, but on friendship. This isn't about denying the power of romantic love; it's about recognizing the underestimated power of platonic connections in building a fulfilling life, and often, a more fulfilling romantic life too.

Think of friendships as the sturdy scaffolding upon which you construct the entire structure of your social life. Romantic relationships, while wonderful, can be inherently volatile. They rise and fall on the tides of passion, shared dreams, and sometimes, even just good hair days. But strong friendships? Those are the bedrock, the reliable support system that's there through thick and thin, the shared laughter echoing through the good times and the comforting presence during the inevitable storms.

The importance of friendship extends far beyond simply having someone to grab coffee with. Strong friendships provide a sense of belonging, a feeling of connection that's crucial for mental and emotional well-being. Studies have shown that individuals with strong social support networks tend to live longer, healthier lives. This isn't just some fluffy self-help trope; there's legitimate scientific backing for the "friends are good for your health" claim. They offer a buffer against stress, a sounding board for ideas, and a much-needed dose of reality when we're trapped in our own self-absorbed narratives (we all have them, let's be honest).

Let's talk about the often-overlooked benefits. Think of the times you've been stuck in a rut, feeling creatively stagnant, or just plain down in the dumps. A good friend can offer a fresh perspective, a kick in the pants (metaphorically, of course, unless they're exceptionally close and you've given them explicit permission to use actual kicks), or simply a listening ear. They see you for who you are, warts and all, and love you anyway.

And this is where the "humorous" part of this self-help guide kicks in. Let's face it, friendships aren't always sunshine and rainbows. They're messy, complicated, and sometimes, downright hilarious. Remember that time you and your best friend accidentally set off the fire alarm at a karaoke night attempting a dramatic rendition of "Bohemian Rhapsody"? Or the time you both got matching, terribly questionable, tattoos on a drunken holiday? Those are the moments that forge the strongest bonds. The shared embarrassments, the inside jokes, the ridiculous adventures—these are the glue that holds friendships together. These shared experiences create a unique tapestry of memories that bind you together, a story only the two of you can tell.

But building those strong friendships requires effort. It's not enough to just sit around and expect friends to magically appear. It's about putting yourself out there, taking the initiative to connect with people who share your interests, values, or at least, your questionable taste in karaoke songs. This might involve joining clubs, volunteering, taking classes, or simply striking up conversations with people you encounter in your daily life. Remember that awkward guy at the gym who always seems to be doing the same workout routine as you? He might be the next best friend you didn't even know existed. I'm not saying start a conversation mid-rep with heavy weights. Choose your moments wisely.

And remember, quality over quantity. A handful of true, supportive friends is far more valuable than a large circle of acquaintances who are just there for the occasional social media likes. Cultivating deep, meaningful friendships requires investment—time, effort, and genuine emotional connection. It's about being present, listening attentively, offering support, and celebrating each other's successes (even the small ones).

Let's address the elephant in the room: conflict. Even the best friendships will experience disagreements. It's inevitable. The key is learning how to navigate these conflicts constructively. Honest communication, empathy, and a willingness to compromise are crucial. It's okay to have different opinions and to disagree; the true strength of a friendship lies in its ability to weather these storms. Just avoid discussing politics, religion, and your deeply held beliefs about the superiority of pineapple on pizza. These are usually guaranteed friendship-enders.

Consider expanding your social circle beyond your immediate group. Challenge yourself to interact with people from diverse backgrounds and experiences. You might discover hidden talents, learn new perspectives, and broaden your horizons in surprising ways. Stepping outside your comfort zone can be daunting, but the rewards are immeasurable.

Think about your existing friendships. Reach out to those you haven't spoken to in a while. A simple phone call, a text message, or an invitation for coffee can rekindle old connections and strengthen bonds. Sometimes, all it takes is a little effort to reignite the spark.

So, how do you cultivate these meaningful platonic connections? It's about being authentic, vulnerable, and willing to be yourself, quirks and all. Don't try to be someone you're not. People are attracted to genuine individuals, those who embrace their imperfections and don't take themselves too seriously. Remember that shared laughter is a powerful bond. Find humor in the everyday, and don't be afraid to be silly.

Cultivating deep friendships takes time, and it's a journey, not a race. It's a continuous process of nurturing the connections you have and creating new ones. Be patient with yourself and with others, and appreciate the beauty of the friendships that enrich your life.

This isn't about ditching romantic pursuits; it's about building a strong foundation of support, laughter, and genuine connection that will enrich all aspects of your life. Think of it as this: strong friendships are like the delicious, perfectly seasoned base of a culinary masterpiece. The romance might be the fancy garnish, the exciting twist, but the delicious base is what keeps it all together and makes it truly satisfying. So, go forth, my friends (platonic and otherwise), and build those connections! You won't regret it. And who knows, maybe you'll find that your next great romantic relationship is already blooming right beside you, disguised as a long-term, hilarious, and entirely irreplaceable friend.

COMMUNITY BUILDING
EXPANDING YOUR SOCIAL CIRCLE

OKAY, SO WE'VE ESTABLISHED that building a robust network of friends is like creating the perfect culinary base for a truly satisfying life. Now, let's get down to the nitty-gritty: how do we actually expand this delicious base? How do we move beyond our existing circle and find those like-minded individuals who will share our joy, endure our questionable karaoke renditions, and maybe even lend a sympathetic ear when we've just endured another disastrous online dating experience (it happens to the best of us).

The truth is, expanding your social circle isn't about some magical formula or a secret handshake. It's about embracing opportunities, stepping outside your comfort zone (yes, I know, the horror!), and remembering that awkward silences are temporary and often followed by surprisingly hilarious moments.

First, let's tackle the elephant in the room: the fear of rejection. We all have it. The imagined scenario of approaching a group of people and being met with stony silence and icy stares is enough to send even the most intrepid social butterfly scurrying back to the safety of their Netflix queue. But here's the thing: most people are far less judgmental than our over-active imaginations would have us believe. They're probably just as nervous about social interactions as you are! The worst that can happen is that they're busy or not interested, and that's okay. It's not a re-flection of your worth; it's simply a matter of timing and compatibility. Think of it as a trial-and-error process, with the occasional hilarious failure to spice things up.

So, where do we even begin? Let's start with the obvious: join a club or group that aligns with your interests. Are you a passionate baker? Join a bread-making club (the aroma alone is worth the price of admission!). A lover of obscure 80s films? Seek out a retro movie night group. A dedicated board game en-thusiast? There's probably a group that plays Settlers of Catan with the intensity of a professional sports team near you. The point is, finding a group centered around a shared passion instantly gives you common ground. It provides a built-in conversation starter (aside from the obvious "Is this sourdough bread as incredible as it smells?").

Beyond clubs, consider taking a class. Whether it's pottery, salsa dancing, or advanced interpretive mime (yes, even that!), learning a new skill provides a fantastic opportunity to meet people with similar interests and a shared willingness to potentially make fools of themselves. The classroom environment is less intimidating than walking up to strangers in a bar. Plus, you have an instant topic of conversation: "Wow, I still haven't mastered the art of the perfectly centered clay pot," or "That salsa move is totally eluding me."

Volunteering is another fantastic avenue. Finding a cause you care about and dedicating some time to it is not only rewarding in itself but also puts you in contact with like-minded individuals. The shared sense of purpose creates an instant bond. It also provides ample opportunities for natural conversation starters: "Wow, I didn't know sorting donations could be so challenging!" or "Have you ever seen someone donate a 50-year-old jar of pickles? It was a masterpiece of preservation!". You never know what comedic gems await you in a volunteer setting.

Now, let's discuss the art of the "casual" encounter. While bar pickups may be the stuff of sitcom legends, the real world offers much more subtle (and often more successful) approaches. Consider striking up conversations with people at the bookstore, coffee shop, or even the park. You know that feeling when you're reading a particularly hilarious passage in a book and you can't help but chuckle aloud? That's your cue! Someone might come along and start up a conversation about the book. It's not a pickup line;

it's a genuine shared appreciation of words. It's organic, genuine, and who knows, it could blossom into an amazing friendship!

This brings me to an important point: be open to meeting people in unexpected places. The gym is an unlikely spot for romance, but often you'll find some quite interesting and engaging people. You can swap tips and complain about exercise equipment. Maybe you'll find a workout buddy and a new friend. Don't be afraid to engage in small talk. You might be surprised at the connections you can forge even during the most mundane activities.

Beyond these tactics, consider leveraging your existing network. Often, the people you know already possess connections you never even considered. That friend-of-a-friend you met at a party? That could be the key to a whole new social circle. Don't be afraid to ask your friends to introduce you to their friends. It takes a little courage, but you may discover an entirely new community that you wouldn't have otherwise stumbled upon. It's the social butterfly effect: one connection could lead to a kaleidoscope of possibilities.

Remember, building meaningful connections takes time and effort. Don't expect to instantly gain a huge group of close friends overnight. It's about nurturing those early interactions, showing genuine interest in others, and being patient. Not every interaction will blossom into a lifelong friendship. And that's okay. Each encounter, whether successful or not, is a step on your journey towards building a rich and fulfilling social life. Embrace the awkwardness, laugh at the inevitable blunders, and remember that the most memorable connections are often the ones that start with a little bit of unexpected chaos. So, go out there, put yourself out there, and start expanding your delicious life base. You might be surprised at what flavors you discover. And hey, even if it doesn't work out romantically, you'll at least have a hilarious story to tell. Trust me, those are priceless.

SELF-IMPROVEMENT
THE FOUNDATION OF HEALTHY
RELATIONSHIPS

SO, YOU'VE BRAVELY ventured forth, armed with witty banter (or at least the intention of witty banter) and a healthy dose of self-deprecating humor, navigating the social landscape in search of meaningful connections. You've added a few delightful spices to your life's culinary base, perhaps even a few unexpected gourmet ingredients. But now, let's talk about the foundation of those delicious relationships: self-improvement. Because let's face it, even the most perfectly crafted soufflé will collapse if the base isn't strong enough.

Building meaningful relationships isn't just about charming people with your dazzling personality (though that certainly helps). It's about cultivating a strong sense of self, understanding your own needs and boundaries, and actively working on becoming the best version of yourself. Think of it as upgrading your social operating system. You wouldn't play the latest video game on a computer from the 1980s, would you? Similarly, you can't expect to thrive in modern relationships without some essential self-improvement upgrades.

First, let's tackle self-awareness. This isn't about navel-gazing to the point of existential crisis; it's about honest self-reflection. What are your strengths? What are your weaknesses? Where do you tend to fall short in social interactions? Are you a master of the accidental foot-in-mouth disease? Do you have a tendency to dominate conversations like a caffeinated octopus on a mission? Are you a chronic latecomer, leaving your friends wondering if you've joined a secret society of time travelers? Identifying these areas is the first step toward improvement. Write them down. Create a personalized "Areas for Improvement" list. Don't be afraid to be brutally honest with yourself; you're not writing this for public consumption. It's your personal guide to becoming a more well-rounded and engaging individual.

Once you've identified your weaknesses, you can start working on them. Maybe you need to work on your active listening skills. Instead of mentally composing your witty retort while someone is speaking, try focusing on what they're saying. It's amazing how much you can learn (and how much more people will enjoy your company) when you genuinely listen.

And please, put the phone down. Unless you're expecting a call from the Nobel Prize committee (in which case, congratulations!), your phone can wait. Perhaps your problem lies in initiating conversations. If so, try starting small. Instead of launching into a complex discussion on the philosophical implications of pineapple on pizza, begin with a simple, genuine compliment or a relevant observation about your shared surroundings. "I love your shoes!" is far less intimidating than "Tell me, what do you think of the inherent absurdity of human existence?" Start with the simpler, more relatable options and slowly expand your conversational range.

If you tend to dominate conversations, practice the art of the graceful pause. Let others chime in. Encourage them to share their thoughts and experiences. Remember, relationships are about reciprocity, not a one-person show. Think of yourself as the conductor of an orchestra, not a solo violinist determined to play every note at deafening volume.

And let's not forget punctuality. Being consistently late shows a lack of respect for other people's time. Aim to be on time or even a few minutes early. If you're consistently late, identify the underlying cause. Is it poor time management? Do you have a peculiar inability to judge how long it takes to get ready? Or are you secretly hoping the people you're meeting will simply forget about you and you can enjoy your own company? Addressing this behavior will not only improve your relationships but it might also save your reputation.

Self-improvement isn't just about fixing flaws; it's also about enhancing your strengths. Are you naturally empathetic? Cultivate that compassion. Are you funny? Develop your comedic timing. Whatever your talents, nurture them. They'll enhance your interactions and make you a more interesting and engaging friend or partner. Think of it as polishing a precious gem. A little extra effort can make a significant difference.

Beyond individual skills, working on your emotional intelligence is crucial. Emotional intelligence involves understanding and managing your own emotions, and recognizing and responding appropriately to the emotions of others. This includes empathy, self-regulation, and social awareness. Someone with high emotional intelligence can navigate difficult conversations, handle conflict constructively, and build strong, supportive relationships. They don't shy away from tough discussions; they confront them directly and thoughtfully.

Imagine two scenarios. In the first, someone expresses frustration about a work project. A person lacking emotional intelligence might respond with a dismissive "Oh, it's not that bad." Someone with high emotional intelligence, however, might say, "That sounds incredibly frustrating. What can I do to help?" See the difference? The first response shuts down the conversation; the second response validates the other person's feelings and shows a willingness to support them.

Another essential aspect of self-improvement is setting healthy boundaries. This means recognizing your limits and communicating them clearly and respectfully. It's okay to say "no" to requests that drain your energy or compromise your values. It's also okay to prioritize your own needs and well-being. Setting healthy boundaries isn't selfish; it's a sign of self-respect. People who consistently overextend themselves often burn out and find themselves with depleted resources, both emotionally and physically. Setting boundaries is the act of self-preservation in the social landscape.

Self-improvement is an ongoing journey, not a destination. It's a continuous process of learning, growing, and refining your skills and understanding of yourself and others. There will be setbacks, moments of self-doubt, and times when you stumble along the way. But the key is to embrace these moments as opportunities for learning and growth. Don't beat yourself up over occasional missteps; learn from them, adjust your approach, and move forward.

Remember the analogy of building a culinary masterpiece? The foundation is critical, and self-improvement forms that very foundation. Without a strong sense of self, a deep understanding of your needs, and a willingness to grow, your relationships are unlikely to reach their full potential. So, invest in yourself. Work on becoming the best version of you. Because the most fulfilling relationships are built not just on shared experiences and laughter, but on a solid base of self-awareness, self-acceptance, and a continuous commitment to self-improvement. And trust me, the result will be a truly delicious and satisfying life. Now, if you'll excuse me, I have some self-improvement work to do... starting with perfecting the art of the graceful exit from overly-long conversations. Wish me luck!

A FINAL WORD
EMBRACING THE JOURNEY

SO, THERE YOU HAVE IT. The grand finale of our whirlwind tour through the often-comical, sometimes chaotic, and always fascinating world of connection-building. We've traversed the landscape of pickup lines (some successful, some spectacularly not), navigated the treacherous waters of awkward silences, and even managed to squeeze in a few insightful reflections on the importance of self-improvement—all while striving to maintain a sense of humor that wouldn't make a seasoned stand-up comedian blush.

But let's be honest, this isn't the end of the story. It's more like the exciting intermission before the next act. Because the journey of connection, my friends, is an ongoing, evolving, and sometimes hilariously unpredictable saga. Think of it less as a destination and more as a wonderfully scenic road trip with unexpected detours, breathtaking vistas, and the occasional flat tire (which, let's face it, is where the truly memorable stories often begin).

This isn't about achieving some mythical state of perfect social mastery. Let's dispense with the illusion that there's some secret formula to instantly become the life of the party or effortlessly attract hordes of admirers. Real life is far more nuanced, more messy, and frankly, a lot funnier than any self-help guru would ever admit. Authentic connection isn't about flawless execution; it's about genuine engagement, vulnerability, and a willingness to embrace the inevitable stumbles along the way.

Remember those cringe-worthy moments we discussed? The disastrous pickup lines? The conversations that went sideways faster than a greased weasel? Don't dismiss them as failures. Consider them valuable lessons disguised in hilariously awkward costumes. They're the comedic relief in the grand narrative of your social evolution, offering invaluable insights into what works (and, more importantly, what spectacularly doesn't). Embrace the absurdity. Laugh at yourself. It's incredibly liberating.

Think of your social life as a never-ending improv show, where you're constantly improvising your way through a series of unscripted scenes. Sometimes you'll nail the punchline; other times, you'll stumble over your words and accidentally trip over the furniture. That's okay. It's the unpredictable nature of the performance that keeps it engaging, keeps it real, and keeps it undeniably funny.

So, how do you keep the momentum going, even when faced with the inevitable awkwardness and occasional social blunders? Here's the secret weapon: persistence. It's not about flawlessly executing every social interaction; it's about consistently showing up, putting yourself out there, and learning from every experience, both the glorious triumphs and the gloriously embarrassing mishaps.

This means actively seeking out opportunities for social interaction. That could involve joining a book club, volunteering for a cause you care about, taking a class on something you've always wanted to learn, leaving a note on a pretty girls bicycle, or simply striking up a conversation with the barista who makes your morning latte (bonus points if you remember their name!). The possibilities are endless, limited only by your imagination (and perhaps your level of caffeine tolerance).

It also means cultivating a mindset of curiosity and openness. Approach new interactions with genuine interest, a willingness to listen, and a desire to learn about others. People are fascinating, complex creatures, each with their own unique stories and perspectives. Engage with them, not as potential conquests or social trophies, but as fellow travelers on this wild and wonderful journey called life.

Don't be afraid to be yourself, quirks and all.

186

Authenticity is magnetic; trying to be someone you're not is exhausting and ultimately ineffective. Embrace your unique brand of humor, your passions, your eccentricities—they're what make you, you. And trust me, people are drawn to genuineness. It's the social equivalent of that perfectly aged cheese: it might be a little pungent, but it's undeniably delicious.

Building meaningful connections is a marathon, not a sprint. There will be days when you feel utterly exhausted, days when you question your social skills, and days when you simply want to curl up on the couch with a bowl of ice cream and a good book (and that's perfectly okay, too!). But the key is to keep moving forward, keep learning, keep growing, and keep that sense of humor intact.

Remember the foundation we talked about in the last chapter? Self-improvement isn't just some abstract concept; it's the fuel that powers your social engine. By continuing to invest in yourself—nurturing your passions, cultivating your strengths, and working on your weaknesses—you'll not only improve your social interactions but enrich your entire life. Think of it as upgrading your social operating system to the latest version. More efficient, more effective, and with significantly fewer glitches.

And finally, remember to celebrate the small victories. That engaging conversation you had with a stranger? The new friend you made at a social gathering? The genuine connection you forged with someone you never thought you'd click with? These are all triumphs, worthy of acknowledgment and celebration. Give yourself credit for showing up, for putting yourself out there, and for actively participating in the ongoing adventure of human connection.

The journey of building meaningful connections is a lifelong pursuit, a never-ending quest for shared laughter, insightful conversations, and enduring friendships. It's a journey filled with unexpected twists, turns, and the occasional spectacularly awkward moment. Embrace the journey, my friends. Embrace the awkwardness. Embrace the laughter. Embrace the incredible, unpredictable, and utterly hilarious adventure of human connection. And remember, even if you trip and fall, at least you'll have a good story to tell (and maybe a few fantastically embarrassing photos to share). So, go forth and connect! The world is waiting (and possibly giggling along with you). The end (for now!). Because, let's be honest, the best stories never truly end. They just pause for an intermission, grab a refill of champagne, and then continue with even more dramatic flair. So, stay tuned... the sequel is already in the works. And it might involve more awkward pickup lines. You've been warned. Or, perhaps more accurately, you've been delightfully forewarned.

ACKNOWLEDGMENTS

FIRST AND FOREMOST, I must thank my incredibly tolerant friends and family. Their unwavering support (and occasional horrified gasps) throughout the writing of this book were invaluable. Special shout-out to my therapist, Dr. Phil (no relation, sadly), for helping me process the sheer volume of dating-related trauma I relived while researching this masterpiece. A heartfelt thank you also goes to my editor, who somehow managed to keep a straight face while reading my more... enthusiastic attempts at humor. Finally, a massive thank you to all the brave souls who unwittingly (or wittingly!) provided the cringe-worthy anecdotes that form the backbone of this book—you know who you are, and I owe you a drink (or maybe therapy).

APPENDIX

THIS APPENDIX CONTAINS a selection of truly awful pickup lines—for educational purposes only, of course. Here are spectacularly terrible pickup lines, guaranteed to make people groan or laugh (but probably not in a good way): Do not attempt to use these on actual human beings. You have been warned. (Seriously, don't. You'll regret it.)

"Are you a parking ticket? Because you've got FINE written all over you."

"Do you have a map? Because I keep getting lost in your eyes. Actually, I'm seriously directionally challenged - could you point me to the exit?"

"If you were a vegetable, you'd be a cute-cumber. Though I suppose you could also be a sweet potato. Or maybe an unusually attractive turnip?"

"Are you French? Because Eiffel for you. I also fell down the stairs earlier, so maybe I just have balance issues."

"Do you believe in love at first sight, or should I walk by again? Actually, I've already walked by 17 times and my feet are getting tired."

"Is your name Google? Because you have everything I've been searching for. Except maybe that weird rash cream I can't find anywhere."

"Are you a magician? Because whenever I look at you, everyone else disappears. Which is actually kind of concerning from a philosophical perspective."

"Do you have a Band-Aid? Because I scraped my knee falling for you. Also, I might have a mild concussion from hitting my head on that doorframe."

"I must be a snowflake, because I've fallen for you. Though technically, I could also be rain. Or hail. Or a very clumsy bird."

"Is your name Wi-Fi? Because I'm really feeling a connection. Though it might just be static electricity from this carpet."

"Do you have a pencil? Because I want to erase your past and write our future. Actually, do you have an eraser? I made some mistakes on this crossword."

"Are you a campfire? Because you are hot and I want s'more. Though I should mention I'm actually allergic to marshmallows."

"If you were a fruit, you'd be a fine-apple. Or possibly a particularly attractive kumquat. I'm not great at fruit analogies."

"Is your dad a boxer? Because you're a knockout!

Wait, is that offensive to assume your parent's profession?"

"Do you believe in destiny? Because I'm pretty sure we were mint to be. That's a pun on 'meant,' by the way. Also, I have some breath mints if you'd like one."

GLOSSARY

Ghosting: The art of mysteriously disappearing from someone's life without explanation. Often practiced by those with questionable social skills (or possibly just a very full schedule).

Friend Zone: A perilous land where romantic hopes and dreams go to die. Avoid at all costs unless platonic friendship is your ultimate goal.

Pickup Line: A verbal attempt to initiate conversation with a potential romantic partner. Success rate highly variable; often inversely proportional to cheesiness.

Rapport: That magical connection you feel with someone—a feeling usually absent in awkward silences.

Cringeworthy: A descriptive term for situations so awkward they induce involuntary muscle spasms. This book contains many examples.

AUTHOR BIOGRAPHY

HECTOR M. RODRIGUEZ is a humorous fiction and non-fiction writer with a background in profound understanding of the complexities (and absurdities) of ancient human interaction. After years of conducting highly unscientific research in bars, coffee shops, and museums (among other less reputable establishments), he decided to compile his findings into this hilariously insightful guide to the art of meeting people. He firmly believes that laughter is the best medicine (and a surprisingly effective social lubricant). When not writing about awkward encounters, he can be found attempting (and often failing) to master the art of the perfectly executed witty banter. He also collects rubber ducks. Don't ask.

REFERENCES

WHILE THIS BOOK is primarily a work of humorous fiction, the following sources provided inspiration and some (very loose) scientific backing for certain claims. Mostly, though, I just made things up.

1. Baumeister, R. F., & Leary, M. R. (1995). The need to belong: Desire for interpersonal attachments as a fundamental human motivation. Psychological bulletin, 117(3), 497.

2. Finkel, E. J., Eastwick, P. W., Karney, B. R., & Reis, H. T. (2012). The psychology of romantic love. Annual review of psychology, 63, 459-489.

3. Various dating apps and websites. (Data gathered through extensive... observation.)

4. G. I. Wanna B. Liked—Life's Inevitable Happening Both Good and Bad. (It's all about balance. 1959.)